A PHILOSOPHY OF TRAGEDY

T0345214

A Philosophy of Tragedy

Christopher Hamilton

REAKTION BOOKS

Published by
Reaktion Books Ltd
Unit 32, Waterside
44–48 Wharf Road
London N1 7UX, UK

www.reaktionbooks.co.uk

First published 2016

Copyright © Christopher Hamilton 2016

All rights reserved

No part of this publication may be reproduced, stored in a retrieval
system, or transmitted, in any form or by any means, electronic,
mechanical, photocopying, recording or otherwise, without the
prior permission of the publishers

Printed and bound in Great Britain
by Bell & Bain, Glasgow

A catalogue record for this book is available from the
British Library

ISBN 978 1 78023 589 9

Man can embody the truth but he cannot know it.
W. B. Yeats

For every age is fed on illusions, lest men should renounce
life early and the human race come to an end.
Joseph Conrad

Contents

Preface

Human beings are born to suffer. All human lives are marked by pain and guilt, by loss and failure, by disappointment and compromise. All of us go through life confused, and need in the end to acknowledge that life itself damages us, often profoundly and always irreparably. Human endeavour is fragile and human beings have only limited control of their own lives. Here and there, there may be progress in one or more senses – moral, political, technological and so on – for some periods, but there is no inevitability about the continuation of such progress. Human nature is not perfectible and happiness is not to be dreamed of – or, rather, is only to be dreamed of – even if there are moments in which we feel happy or content. Our desires are often in conflict with each other, and our reason is a fragile instrument that is largely driven by blind urges and needs. There is no moral world order; the wicked often flourish while the good are crushed and perish. Most of the time we do not really understand what we are doing, and there is no goal or purpose to history and no redemption for our pain and suffering. Human beings think they long for contentment, but when they get it they often destroy it because they are creatures who are deeply divided against themselves. And however excellent or morally good a life one has led, it ends in death, which is final, and from which there is no release or redemption.

If human life is as I have just described it then the human condition is tragic. This is the point of view that I offer in this book.

* ✳ *

There are other ways of thinking of tragedy: there is that which we find in the tragic theatre in the plays of Aeschylus and Sophocles, of Shakespeare and Racine, and in the modern tragedies of, say, Büchner and Chekhov; and there is the notion we have in mind when we say that the death of the little girl in the swimming pool was a tragedy, or the sudden and unexpected collapse of the athlete while running was a tragedy. I shall draw on such notions of tragedy in this book, but my focus will be on tragedy in the sense of something that describes our fundamental condition.

It will be clear from what I have said that, from this point of view, human beings are not at home in the world: we are like wanderers on the face of an earth wholly indifferent to us. This has always been so, but this homelessness speaks with special clarity to certain ages, ages in which old ways of dealing with, of making sense of, the tragic condition of human beings seem increasingly implausible or in-credible. Ours is such an age. It is so because, for many, it is no longer possible to believe in an overarching moral-metaphysical system that makes sense of our life, such as Christianity – my focus here, though what I say also applies in various ways to many other forms of religious faith – which can only appear, from the present perspective, as a kind of elaborate system of denial of the truth about our condition.

For, after all, Christianity claims that, rightly understood, we are at home in the world, even if 'world' here includes a goal or end point that stretches beyond our earthly existence. As the philosopher Rush Rhees remarked:

> To look on it as God's world – the religious view of the
> world – is to . . . have some sense, however indefinite
> (and it may be deep for all that) of the world, the way
> things happen, as expressing the will of God: that even
> in tragedy one can see something: sense of the eternal
> which one does not understand.[1]

Christianity – of which there are many varieties, not always
in agreement with each other – says, at least in certain of its
central manifestations, that there is a moral world order, that,
in the final analysis, the good will flourish and be happy and
the wicked will be punished or otherwise reap the reward of
their wickedness. It offers a vision of (moral) progress which
issues in redemption for individuals and human beings as
such. It tells us that we are fallen creatures, fundamentally
broken in some deep metaphysical and psychological sense,
tainted by original sin, and that we are in this sense in conflict
with ourselves, but it claims that there is a final redemption
from this in God's forgiving love. So, even if we are born to
suffer, as Christianity has often acknowledged, this suffering
has a meaning and a purpose, the central image of which is
Jesus on the cross. It says that, even if we often lack self-
knowledge, God knows us completely and cares for us. And
it claims that, even if human beings (often) lack control over
their lives, God ultimately has a plan for the course of human
history and for each human life, such that individual lives and
human history possess an order which God can see clearly
and we can discern darkly.

But for many these claims are no longer credible. The
discoveries of Darwin, the advance of scientific knowledge
of human beings and our understanding of the planet we
live on, the unspeakable barbarities that took place during
the twentieth century, the historicized consciousness of the
modern mind, and other things besides, give force to the
idea, articulated by Max Weber, that we live in a world that

is *entzaubert*, disenchanted. This is why I think of a book on tragedy as timely.

This book, then, aims to explore this tragic condition of humanity and it does so from a philosophical point of view. What I try to do in this book is explore a number of connected themes that illuminate this condition. In doing so I aim to provide what one might call a hermeneutic of the tragic: the project is to articulate a specific perspective on the world that, while seeking to express something fundamental about our permanent condition, might nonetheless speak especially to the modern sceptical spirit. The tragic perspective offered here is, in the light of the collapse of the old metaphysical and moral certainties, culturally available to us in an especially clear way, and may resonate for many who reflect on their hitherto not fully articulated sense of how things hang together (or fail to do so) for them. In this sense, this book is an attempt to take seriously Nietzsche's idea of the death of God: what, it asks, does the world look like if one seeks fully to accept that idea, not simply as a philosophical or intellectual puzzle, but as a real existential question?

It should be clear from even the little that I have said so far that I do not share the view of the so-called 'new atheists' who think of religion, and Christianity in particular, as some kind of historical error, a confused, pre-scientific attempt to understand the world, which has now been replaced by science and modern moral thinking and from which we are lucky to be free. I do not think Christianity is foolish or childish and I believe that it saw the tragedy of our condition clearly. To this extent, it tells the truth. However, its preferred solutions to that tragedy are no longer, in my view, credible, for the reasons I have already given. If science contributes to this, it is not because science disproves Christianity. It is because it forms just part of a massive cultural shift that makes Christianity implausible to many.

For although there are, no doubt, parts of science that are in conflict with Christianity, Auschwitz, in my view, gives more reason than any scientific advance or discovery to disbelieve in God.

I am well aware that there are, perhaps particularly among philosophers, some highly sophisticated versions of Christianity that seek to make it compatible with the modern, sceptical consciousness by dispensing, to a greater or lesser extent, with the very idea that Christianity does or ought to demand intellectual assent to specific propositions, specific statements of belief. Christianity from this view is not about what one believes but about praxis, about the life one leads. There is much to be said for these approaches and they are helpful in dispelling absurd and simplistic misconceptions about Christianity. Nonetheless, although I cannot argue this here in detail, I do not think they succeed: in the end they trade upon a conception of Christianity that they reject in order to make their claims comprehensible and, while they may offer various forms of salutary and much-needed spiritual discipline, such discipline is better and more honestly found in alternative traditions, such as Buddhism.

The tragic view of life I offer here is not intended to be the only form that such a view could take; there may be other ways of thinking of life as tragic – related ways, no doubt, but not exactly the same as that which I outline here. Nor, therefore, is what I say intended to capture the only way in which philosophers and others have thought about the notion of tragedy; there is, indeed, no one such thing we mean by 'tragedy' and I have no ambition to say that the term should be used only in the way I use it. Nevertheless, I hope that I am able to capture something like a central perspective on tragedy as it has been explored in philosophy, literature and life.

Introduction: Philosophy and Tragedy: A Personal View

There is a moment in Sándor Márai's novel *The Rebels*, set at the time of the Great War, in which one of the young people at the centre of the story, Ábel, who has begun to be interested in books and in the act of writing, finds himself astonished at such things:

> What does it mean when a man picks up a pen and writes something? When something simply comes to him and it appears there, complete, in his writing? Why should he have done that? Is this what writers do? He had come across a book once that someone had brought home from the front. It was a Russian book, full of Russian script. A novel. The author was anonymous. He could not help but feel shaken at the thought of it. Somewhere in Russia there lived this anonymous figure conjuring characters, events, and entire tragedies out of nothing, committing them to paper, a spirit floating over an immense distance, and here he was holding it in his hands.
>
> . . .
>
> Books hide some secret, not precisely in what they said, but in the reason for them being written at all . . . What he wanted to know was why books existed.[1]

Ábel's worry here may seem very strange, as if it were a worry about something that really is not a puzzle at all. But there *is* something very odd about the existence of books. You might be struck by that at any moment.

Recently I was in a bookshop. I picked up a book by Jean Guéhenno. I had never heard of him before and knew nothing about him. I do not know why I picked up that book in particular. It was pure chance. I started looking through it and found it fascinating. Suddenly, this person Guéhenno existed for me. And I for him. I seemed to possess him and he me. Here was someone of whose existence I had known nothing. Then, by chance, he seemed important to me. It was as if the book had been lying in wait for me to pick it up, as if Guéhenno himself had been waiting for me, patiently biding his time among all the others on those shelves. And it really was as if he came to me like a spirit, floating over the distance, as Márai says. Had he never written the book, I would still know nothing of him. But if he had written it and I had not picked it up, it would be as if his spirit were somehow calling out to me but I could not hear.

In his reflection 'Borges and I' Jorge Luis Borges writes:

It is to the other Borges that things happen. By mail I receive news of Borges, and I see his name on a shortlist of academics or in a biographical dictionary . . . It would be an exaggeration to say that our relationship is hostile; I live, I let myself live, so that Borges can weave his literature, and that literature is my justification. I gladly admit that he has managed to write certain sound pages, but those pages cannot save me . . . I am definitively destined to oblivion, and only fleeting moments of me will be able to survive in the other man . . . So my life is a fugue, and I lose everything, and everything belongs to oblivion, or to the other man.

I am not sure which of the two is writing this page.[2]

Among the many questions these examples impress upon one concerning the strangeness of books, the two most direct are: who is writing? And for whom?

The poet, said W. B. Yeats, 'is never the bundle of accident and incoherence that sits down to breakfast; he has been reborn as an idea, as something intended, complete.'[3] This may be true of any writer, I suppose. It is certainly true of the philosopher. The conflicted mess of what he is, the confusions that make up his life, the trivialities and banalities that pursue him and with which he pursues himself – these are not to be seen in the organized lines of reflection and argument that make up the philosophical text.

Yet the philosopher can ask himself or herself: who am I as I write this? With what part of me, out of which of my confusions and better insights, do I write? What parts of my experience and temperament am I willing to put into this piece of writing, what part of it do I wish to avoid and what part of it is unknowingly or unconsciously deflected?

Philosophers do not usually ask themselves these questions. They would, in general, consider them out of place in philosophy. For philosophy deals, many would say, in questions of the logical relations between concepts, objective questions about the mind or knowledge and the like, and these are impersonal issues, unconnected with the philosopher's inner life.

Perhaps there are parts of philosophy that are impersonal in this way. But when the topic is the tragic condition of humanity it is hard to believe that the kinds of questions I have raised can be irrelevant, because it is hard to believe that a tragic sense of life could be one of those impersonal philosophical questions. No one comes to the idea that the human condition is tragic by being convinced by a philosophical argument, and, although the philosophical reflections of others inform one's thinking here, as elsewhere, it is clear that what brings one to such a view, if anything does, is life itself, the things that happen to one, the things one does and the things one sees in oneself and others.

In such cases as these, the philosopher is not what Miguel de Unamuno called a 'pretext':

> In most of the histories of philosophy that I know, philosophic systems are presented to us as if growing out of one another spontaneously, and their authors, the philosophers, appear only as mere pretexts. The inner biography of the philosophers, of the men who philosophized, occupies a secondary place. And yet it is precisely this inner biography that explains for us most things.[4]

It is not simply philosophical argument that is at stake here. Rather, one's existence as a human being is implicated. This is what Unamuno meant by reminding us that the philosopher is not an abstract intelligence, but a man or woman of flesh and bone. Montaigne, one the greatest and least illusioned of Renaissance thinkers, would add, of sweat, tears, blood and shit.

Iris Murdoch said that it is always appropriate to ask of the philosopher: what is he afraid of?[5] That could be intended as a remark about purely intellectual fears, fears that do not engage the human being. But Murdoch intended it as a reminder that the philosopher's humanity is invested in his or her philosophy. Almost alone among contemporary philosophers, Michael McGhee, in his fine book *Transformations of Mind*, asks himself Murdoch's question:

> It has been an abiding fear of mine, that the state of my own humanity, the way I think and feel, the way I *act*, or fail to act (soured by my deeds), may also affect, adversely, my philosophy, my capacity to see, to see error, to see ordinary truths.[6]

A philosopher's thinking can be deflected by, deformed by, his failings as a human being. But his failings as a human being may be part of what makes urgent the need for philosophical reflection in the first place. The state of McGhee's humanity may have adversely affected his philosophy, but it also is part of what makes his philosophy so valuable.

A philosopher's thinking can be deflected too by his desire, although it may not be fully acknowledged, to arrive at the conclusion he wants to get to and avoid conclusions he finds unpleasant. Robert Nozick *did* acknowledge that – a very rare exception among philosophers: 'My concern is not only intense, but directed.' He wondered whether other philosophers were more dispassionate than he was, less invested in getting to a particular conclusion. He did not think so:

A philosopher's concerns are exhibited within his work on a topic as well as in selecting that topic. When a philosopher sees that premises he accepts logically imply a conclusion he has rejected until now, he faces a choice: he may accept this conclusion, or reject one of the previously accepted premises, or even postpone the decision about which to do. His choice will depend on which is greater, the degree of his commitment to the various premises or the degree of his commitment to denying the conclusion. It is implausible that these are independent of how strongly he wants certain things to be true. The various means of control over conclusions explain why so few philosophers publish ones that (continue to) upset them. I do not recall any philosopher reporting in distress that on some fundamental question he is forced to conclude that the truth is awful, worse even than the third best he would want it to be.[7]

Does that not render the argument worthless? Nozick, surely correctly, thought not. We can learn things along the way, he said, as we move towards the conclusion. Further, while the general shape of the conclusion may be known from the outset, its specific contours may not be. They become clear as things go on.

Still, it is very strange, as Nozick says, that so much philosophy is coercive or like war.[8] He writes:

> The terminology of philosophical art is coercive: arguments are *powerful* and best when they are *knockdown*, arguments *force* you to a conclusion, if you believe the premisses you *have to* or *must* believe the conclusion, some arguments do not carry much *punch*, and so forth. A philosophical argument is an attempt to get someone to believe something, whether he wants to believe it or not. A successful philosophical argument, a strong argument, *forces* someone to a belief.[9]

Despite this, as Nozick says, if a person 'is willing to bear the label of "irrational" or "having the worse arguments", he can skip away happily maintaining his previous belief'. Nozick goes on:

> Wouldn't it be better if the philosophical arguments left the person no possible answer at all, reducing him to impotent silence? . . . Perhaps philosophers need arguments so powerful they set up reverberations in the brain: if the person refuses to accept the conclusion, he *dies*.[10]

This is very odd. The philosopher writes an argument, getting to a conclusion he wants to get to, and then seeks to get others to believe it whether they want to or not. What is he afraid of? Why does he want others to agree with him?

Perhaps, as I said, there are some parts of philosophy that are impersonal, where the philosopher's desires and fears, his humanity, are irrelevant to his thinking, to his arguments. I am not sure, though I feel confident that if there are such they occupy a much smaller part of philosophy than is usually supposed. Be that as it may, in those parts of philosophy in which one's humanity is invested in one's thinking, it would surely be important to make clear in what way this is so, if only in the name of honesty. It is very rare for a philosopher to seek to do that. Usually the invitation is resisted, even if it is noticed. There is not the vocabulary available in philosophy for doing this; it is a discipline that has developed largely without paying a great deal of attention to the challenge. There are exceptions, of course; Montaigne is one such. But such cases are rare.

Philosophy seems to be haunted by the idea that the only alternative to an impersonal way of proceeding is some kind of unwarranted or self-indulgent self-referentiality, as if one had no choice other than that between impersonality or auto-biography. But this cannot be right. We need to distinguish between speaking personally and speaking *merely* personally. As an example of the former, we might turn to Samuel Johnson, who had an extraordinary ability to take his personal experiences, fears, confusions and the like and make from them a conception of man's tragic condition that resonates with the rest of us. As Arieh Sachs has said of Johnson:

> The natural movement of his mental processes was to follow upon and generalize from highly personal experience, so that all his ideas about the general human situation are in a very important sense an extension of private sensibility . . . Johnson's greatness lies in his ability to transmute his personal distress of melancholy, guilt and indolence into impersonal observation.[11]

Impersonal observation in this context clearly does not mean observation unconnected with the inner life of the thinker;

quite the contrary. It means that the observations express the thinker's humanity but are not *merely* personal: they depend upon his sensibility and are shot through with it, but they are not *about* that sensibility.

A way of writing and speaking in philosophy that seeks to acknowledge the thinker's desires and fears in his reflections should not be *about* those desires and fears. Rather, what is required is a style of writing that resists the temptation to complete impersonality – a fear of metaphor and imagination, a reduced conceptual repertoire, an attachment to the literal-minded, all of which are typical of much philosophical writing – while being disciplined in various ways, for example, through engagement with what others have had to say on the subject; by seeking to bear in mind that one's failings of character might deform one's thinking; and by trying to 'go the bloody hard way', as Ludwig Wittgenstein recommended to his students they should, resisting if one can sentimentality and cheap consolation.

The kind of approach in question also requires that one seek to resist the typical coerciveness of philosophy, which, from the present perspective, can only be one more expression of the refusal of one's weakness and one's humanity. The aim, rather, is for a kind of meditative, open-ended style of reflection that is aware of its incompleteness. Socrates said that a problem with any given book is that it says the same thing to each person who reads it, regardless of the individual subjectivity of the reader. He preferred conversation, believing that this opened up the interlocutors better to each other. One sees the point, though there are plenty of people who are coercive in conversation. 'For whom does one write?', cannot be answered with 'Everyone', though much philosophical writing seems to have some such sense of itself in mind since, as Nozick pointed out, 'works of philosophy are written as though their authors believe them to be the absolutely final word on their subject',[12] which is certainly true of a great deal of philosophy. Nozick himself, worried by the patterns of domination that are implicitly set up between writer and reader, wrote: 'I place no extreme obligation of attentiveness on my readers; I hope instead for those who read as I do, seeking what they can learn from, make use of, transform for their own purposes.'[13] It is extremely hard to write in the light of the generosity of that sentiment, but it is the right one, I think.

Perhaps most importantly, if one is to write as a philosopher knowing that one is not a mere pretext, it is crucial to bear in mind the distinction between what one *thinks one thinks* and what one *really thinks*. We all think we think certain things that we do not really think. We do this for all kinds of reasons: because we wish to present ourselves as being more coherent, less inconsistent than we are; because we wish to appear morally better than we are; because we are too lazy to think about what we really think, or because it is just too exhausting to do so; because we respond according to our expectations of what we suppose others want to hear; because we are frightened or intimidated by our interlocutor; because we wish to appear more intelligent than we know ourselves to be; and much else besides. One of the most difficult things to do is to find out what one really thinks, and I am certainly not the first to believe that a great deal of human speech, including intellectual discourse, has the secret aim of allowing its participants to conceal from themselves and from each other what they really think.

The struggle to say what one really thinks, and not to rest content with what one thinks one thinks, is a demand on one's humanity, understood as something to whose requirements one has to rise. Humanity in this sense is something one has; but it is also, more importantly, a kind of achievement.

It goes without saying that this is a phenomenally difficult task, not just because it is so difficult to know what might fulfil it, but because it is profoundly difficult even to get the nature of the task in focus. At a general or abstract level one can hope for nothing more than 'hints and guesses, / Hints followed by guesses', to use T. S. Eliot's words from 'The Dry Salvages' in a different context. There is no substitute for example, as in Johnson. The difficulty of even knowing what the task is makes it much easier simply to retreat into a style of writing that seems to offer protection by seeking to be wholly impersonal, unconnected with the thinker's humanity. This is one of the sources of the aridity of much philosophical writing, and it is one of the reasons that many people often find the style of the subject rebarbative.

But if the task in question is difficult at the best of times and can only be fulfilled partially and with much hesitancy, the situation is aggravated if one is seeking to speak about the tragic condition of human beings. This is because tragedy, whatever else it is, is disruptive. It is a form of, or represents a form of, disruption, chaos and disorder: suffering, loss, senselessness and so on. But philosophy keeps that disorder at a distance. It does this in the person of the philosopher and in what the philosopher says.

For, as I write this, I feel wholly or, at any rate, sufficiently insulated, in this moment, from the tragedy of life, as does what I write. How could it be otherwise? How could I write unless I felt this way? To write as I am now doing requires me to be calm, reflective, judicious. These are virtues that philosophy prizes and I have done my best to cultivate them, at least when I am doing philosophy. But when I am angry or melancholy, or feeling wretched or bloody and hate the world and myself for its, my, stupidity and folly, well *then* I am not much good at doing philosophy, but *then* I feel the sense of the tragedy of things flow through me. Martha Nussbaum, reflecting on her own work in the philosophy of tragedy, makes a similar point. Speaking of various lectures she gave on the topic, lectures that then became part of one of her books, she writes:

For as the writer and speaker of the lectures I felt myself to be not at all passively vulnerable to fortune . . . It occurred to me to ask myself whether the act of writing about the beauty of human vulnerability is not, paradoxically, a way of rendering oneself less vulnerable, and more in control of the uncontrolled elements in life.[14]

The answer is that it is.

If the philosopher's humanity is caught up in the text he writes about tragedy, as I have suggested it is, then that humanity is, so to speak, betrayed by the demands the philosopher makes on himself to write and by what the text can hope to provide. Tragedy is destructive both of the philosopher's inner equilibrium as he writes and of the order that the philosopher must introduce into his reflections to make them as clear and as cogent as possible. If life is tragic, then philosophy is not somehow immune to that. Yet the very writing of a philosophy of tragedy must be done, cannot but be done, from a position that intimates immunity. To that extent, it must fail.

This is the basic outlook of this book: life is itself tragic and cannot be understood philosophically. In this sense, this book is a kind of impossibility. It tries to articulate something that cannot be articulated. How are we to understand this? My suggestion is that we think of what follows in the book as a series of gestures towards something which cannot be fully articulated. They might also be hints or signs. They trace something that cannot be fully said.

Yet, even if I were able to provide more than gestures, whether you agree with what is said in this book will depend a great deal on your temperament and experiences, on your sense of yourself as a person. I said earlier that no one comes to believe that the human condition is tragic on the basis of a philosophical argument. If you agree with what I say here, it will not be because I have given you good arguments to agree with me but because the book articulates something that you are inclined to accept anyway, or seems to ring true with you. For if you are inclined to find life tragic you might find that my articulation of that idea captures something of your sense of things. Of course, you almost certainly would not have put things exactly as I have, or you might want to add something to what I say, but that is how it should be, since nothing in what I can say here could be the definitive truth, as if I might have had the ambition to say all that could be said on the matters with which this book deals – which of course I do not.

In truth I cannot offer you anything more than what the philosopher and psychologist William James called an 'individual way of just seeing and feeling the total push and pressure of the cosmos', my 'sense of what life honestly and deeply means'.[15] Any philosophy that offers a vision of the world and our place in it does this. And you will bring your vision of things to your reflection on what I have to say here.

To offer such a vision is, however, a deeply problematic undertaking. The reason for this is that one offers it as the truth, as the right or correct way of looking at and experiencing the world. And yet one knows it cannot be.

We can see this clearly by adverting to something that came up in an interview with Philip Larkin, conducted by John Haffenden. During the interview, Haffenden quoted the end of Larkin's poem 'Dockery and Son':

> Life is first boredom, then fear.
> Whether or not we use it, it goes,
> And leaves what something hidden from us chose,
> And age, and then the only end of age.

Then the conversation went as follows:

Haffenden: What do you say to your critics who imply or infer that at some point you predetermined what you felt about life, that you made up your mind once and for all, for example, about the occasions of suffering that people endure?

Larkin: They've got it the wrong way round. I don't decide what I think about life: life decides that, either through heredity or environment, what you're born with or what happens to you. If I'd been born a different person and different things had happened to me, I might have written differently. I didn't invent age and death and failure and all that, but how can you ignore them?
. . .

Haffenden: Isn't there a danger in adducing one's own temperament as the truth about life?

Larkin: A danger for who [*sic*]? Nobody pays any attention to what you write. They read it and then forget about it. There may be a lunatic fringe who believe that life is what writers say, not what they experience themselves, but most people just say, 'Oh well, that's what it's like to be Larkin', and start thinking about something else.

Haffenden: And yet, to go back to the sort of statement you make at the end of 'Dockery and Son': you see it as true, but others might dispute it.

Larkin: It's a bit simplified, I suppose, but I think it's all perfectly true. I can't see how anyone could possibly deny it, any of it.[16]

Larkin knows two things: first, that his own view is nothing more than that, his own view, dependent upon his own experiences, temperament and the rest; second, that he cannot see how anyone could deny it, that is, that it is true and should be accepted by everyone else.

I know also of my view of the world what Larkin knows of his, and you know it of yours. First, I have thought about my view on things and I can give reasons for looking at the world as I do look at it. That is what I shall be doing in the rest of this book. That giving of reasons seems to imply that you ought to agree with me. After all, that is what I seem to be doing in giving reasons. But second, I also know that what I think depends deeply on my own temperament and my own experiences and, in this sense, I know that what I believe is contingent, a matter of chance and luck, good and bad, of who I happen to be and what has chanced to happen to me.

Each of us is caught in the toils of the fact that we possess, or are possessed by, our own vision of the way the world is, and have also what we take to be good reasons for that view, yet know, if we are honest, that what we believe is profoundly contingent, dependent on the vagaries of our individual temperament and experiences. So we know that we would have thought something quite different if we had had a different temperament or different experiences or both, just as Larkin says, and would have given what would seem to be good reasons for *that* view. One's reasons, when one reflects on them in this way, seem to crumble away into the mere contingency of one's simply *happening* to believe these things. Truth seems to be, from this point of view, elusive.

This invites one into a kind of vertigo, a sense that, however convinced one might be of one's own position, whatever reasons one has or takes oneself to have for what one thinks, it rests, in the end, on nothing, floating in the air free from any foundation that might support it. It also demands of one a kind of spiritual discipline. The Franco-Romanian philosopher Emil Cioran pointed out that man is the dogmatic animal par excellence, seemingly possessed of, or rather by, a natural tendency to convert what he believes into things that others ought to accept: we are all of us potential fanatics. The sense of vertigo in question demands of one the spiritual discipline to resist converting what one believes into what others should accept too.

On this view, there might be something that for a given individual is his or her truth, his or her way of truthfully living a life, but there is no such thing as *the* truth, no such thing as the uniquely *right* or *correct* way of looking at life. You can look at life as tragic or comic; as an adventure or as a trial; as an arena in which we are carried by, but also tested by, God's love; as a struggle between fundamentally egotistical individuals; as a scene of amusement and joy; as a kind of pantomime or as more of a farce; and so on. P. F. Strawson in one of his philosophical essays speaks of other such possibilities, of

> the ideas of self-obliterating devotion to duty or to the service of others; of personal honour and magnanimity; of asceticism, contemplation, retreat; of action, dominance and power; of the cultivation of 'an exquisite sense of the luxurious'; of simple human solidarity and co-operative endeavour; of a refined complexity of social existence; of a constantly maintained and renewed affinity with natural things.[17]

Strawson says that here there are truths, but no truth. I would make the same point by saying that each of these ways could be a way for some individuals to live a life truthfully, and people can have good reasons for what they think and feel, for living in *that* way. No doubt different individuals' views overlap in various ways and can find points of shared or common ground. But, in the end, I am suggesting that there is no way of justifying one or other of these ways of living as *the* correct or right way to live.

The great philosophers – Plato, Aristotle, Spinoza, Hume, Kant, Schopenhauer, Heidegger and so on – each express a possible vision of life, and the lesser philosophers seek protection and justification, knowingly or not, in such visions. Sometimes the technical arguments of such philosophers might seem to have no connection with such visions, but they lurk in the background, often unnoticed because they are widely accepted and thus pass unseen. And the vision itself is just that, a vision, and cannot, as a whole, be justified or refuted. This is one reason why, despite two and a half thousand years of Western philosophy, philosophers have not arrived at agreement on any of the major questions they discuss. While they take themselves to be seeking for the truth, what they end up doing is elaborating a vision of the world. Those elaborating other visions also take themselves to be seeking for the truth. But, in reality, they are to a greater or lesser extent, despite any overlaps in vision there might be, doing different things, working on and within different visions of the world. Were this not the case it would be impossible to see why philosophers are not better at finding the truth than they are. But on the view I am urging, each great philosopher offers us a vision of the world as each great novelist or playwright does, and we can enter these worlds imaginatively but prove none of them; this is why we speak of the world in Conrad's vision, or that of D. H. Lawrence or Henry James or George Eliot or Jane Austen. And we can do the same with the philosophers: Kant's world is not that of Aristotle, or that of Plato or Nietzsche or Hume and so on. In this way at least, philosophy is a form of literature, a point that has been made by very few philosophers,[18] but which has been either fiercely resisted or (usually) just ignored by them otherwise.

We come back, then, to Nozick's point about the philosopher's unacknowledged desire to get to his preferred conclusions. That desire is expressed in the visions of the world that different philosophers offer. James makes the point elegantly:

> The history of philosophy is to a great extent that of a certain clash of human temperaments . . . Of whatever temperament a professional philosopher is, he tries when philosophizing to sink the fact of his temperament. Temperament is no conventionally recognized

reason, so he urges impersonal reasons only for his conclusions. Yet his temperament really gives him a stronger bias than any of his more strictly objective premises. It loads the evidence for him one way or the other, making for a more sentimental or a more hard-hearted view of the universe, just as this fact or that principle would. He *trusts* his temperament. Wanting a universe that suits it, he believes in any representation of the universe that does suit it.

Yet in the forum he can make no claim, on the bare ground of his temperament, to superior discernment or authority. There thus arises a certain insincerity in our philosophic discussions: the potentest of all our premises is never mentioned.[19]

I said earlier that there may be parts of the philosopher's work that are genuinely impersonal or some philosophical topics which really are purely conceptual matters and have no connection with the inner life of the philosopher. But if there are such, the visions of the world that philosophers offer are not part of them.

Philosophy is entangled in our humanity, and yet longs to leave that behind: this is its investment in the impersonal and the wholly objective, freed from all connection with the inner life of the philosopher. It expresses in this way one of the permanent hopes, or fantasies, of human beings: the desire to transcend our humanity, to leave behind our weakness and confusion, our partiality and limited visions. It cannot do this, but its desire to do so is the central reason why philosophy constantly needs to be recalled to face up to our humanity instead of hiding from it, fleeing it.

But that recall always comes too late. This is because it just is part of our condition as human beings to wish to escape that condition. Philosophy is not, in that sense, an aberration. Between its longing to escape our humanity and the need to be recalled, or to recall itself, to our humanity, it plays out a fundamental feature of our life: there is no such thing as an acceptance of our humanity because our humanity is constituted by a longing to transcend it. Human beings exist in deep contradiction with themselves. They cannot bear themselves and they flee themselves even as they seek to understand themselves. This is central to their tragic consciousness.

Because this consciousness cannot be fully articulated, cannot get itself clearly in its own view, fleeing itself as it seeks itself, the concept of *mood* is central in expressing it. It is characteristic of a mood that it intimates to us an experience of the way things are – of reality – as a whole, and that it does so in an immediate, non-discursive sense, that is, in a way that resists full articulation in conceptual terms. It is for this reason that it is often through music that one may feel that a sense of the tragic nature of life can be articulated. Music – one might think of, say, Shostakovich's String Quartet No. 13 in B flat minor (Opus 138) – can, on occasion, intimate a distinctive *mood* that we might think of as, experience as, tragic, but what that mood is cannot be articulated beyond that: it can be heard only in the music. Similarly if we think that a play expresses a tragic sense of life, we might suggest that it is the distinctive *mood* of the play that does this and that this mood is something that the play invites us into in virtue of the things it says, its language, its characters and so on, but which exceeds or goes beyond that explicit content. A mood pervades or colours experience in a distinctive way – it gives to it what philosophers call a specific phenomenology – and it is also characteristic of a mood that it can come into and go out of focus, can wax and wane. This is why someone who thinks that life is tragic does not, or, at any rate, need not, exist permanently in the mood which is the tragic mood, that is, be in a state in which he permanently experiences the world as tragic. Rather, he will think that this mood is the most revelatory of the way the world is and that when he experiences this mood, in one or more of the many ways in which a mood can be experienced, reality most deeply reveals itself to him as it is. After all, this is typical of moods: we do not, in general, trust all of our moods as revealing to us correctly the way things are since we know them to be passing and we suppose that some are more reliable in this regard.

The tragic mood, precisely because it is at once elusive in conceptual terms, yet so intimate and powerful in its phenomenology, in its appearance in consciousness, has a certain opacity that is, nonetheless, experienced as deeply revelatory. This is, I am suggesting, of a piece with the elusiveness of humanity to itself. At the individual level, that elusiveness or opacity is expressed as a basic orientation towards the world, an 'attunement' to use a term of Heidegger's, which cannot be fully described and whose reason for being as it is escapes us. Larkin expressed that idea by saying that one does not decide what one thinks about life; life decides that through one. We can bring it yet more sharply into focus by considering a further example, that of the different characters in Virginia Woolf's novel *The Waves*.

There are seven characters in the novel, six of whom speak, but what we are provided with is nothing resembling conversation. Rather, we are confronted with the characters' various internal monologues, the ways they have of thinking the world, feeling the world, their experience of their environment – or, better, of themselves in their environment – and so on. From the first we are aware of their immense difference from each other, of the way in which they are each attuned to the world in a very particular way that defines who they are and what their life is. Bernard is a storyteller, in love with words, descriptions, and spinning narratives and anecdotes from encounters with the people around him. He knows that 'Louis and Neville [two other characters in the novel] . . . feel the presence of other people as a separating wall. But I find myself in company with other people' and he feels that 'there is about both Neville and Louis a precision, an exactitude, that I admire and shall never possess'. Neville, who is homosexual, is an aesthete, in love with poetry and beguiled by the image of lazing on the grass with the Latin poets. Yet despite all this – or perhaps because of this – he feels that 'there is some flaw in me – some fatal hesitancy, which, if I pass it over, turns to foam and falsity'. Louis is an outsider because he is a foreigner among the English, who seeks acceptance from others and always feels excluded. Jinny is all body, narcissistic and craves the attention of others, especially men, to her as the body she is. Susan loves the earth and hates the city, feels deeply alienated from man's urban existence and is profoundly attached to the land and the rhythms of the seasons. Rhoda is a loner, troubled by life, disturbed in the depths of her being. She tells herself at one point that she will seek to 'put off [her] . . . hopeless desire to be Susan, to be Jinny', a desire born of her longing to escape from the fact that, as she says of herself, 'There is some check in the flow of my being'.[20]

It is clear that Woolf intends these features of each character to be gestures towards, indications of or hints concerning the fundamental orientation towards life, the basic attunement of each of these individuals. And for our purposes there are two key things to be noticed. First, what any given person's orientation is is itself not wholly clear. As in the case of Woolf's characters, we can have nothing but gestures towards that, more or less helpful or insightful as the case may be, but gestures nonetheless. Second, there is no explanation for why a given individual has the orientation he has. In the end, there is no explanation for why each of us is as we are. We just find that we are as we are, as if there were some basic metaphysical fact about who we are that eludes all choice and all consciousness. The attunement we each have towards the world is not something for which we can provide reasons; we are left with the mysterious fact that one is as one is. A fundamental opacity attends who one is.

It is for this reason, I think, that one must remain forever dislocated from both oneself and the world. It is this kind of tragic insight which can give us the sense that, somehow or other, whatever it is that one does in life, one in some way misses what is essential to living. This, I think, is expressed, for example, in Kathleen Raine's comment that 'our lives are encumbered with irrelevancies which we mistake for living experience, and which in the end come more and more to usurp it.'[21] And occasionally we get a glimpse of this, of the strange way in which we are cut off from, or dislocated from, what Raine calls 'living experience'. Georg Lukács describes it thus:

> Real life is always unreal, always impossible, in the midst of empirical life. Suddenly there is a gleam, a lightening that illuminates the banal paths of empirical life: something disturbing and seductive, dangerous and surprising; the accident, the great moment, the miracle; an enrichment and a confusion. It cannot last, no one would be able to bear it, no one could live at such heights – at the height of their own life and their own ultimate possibilities. One has to fall back into numbness. One has to deny life in order to live.[22]

But we can never say exactly *what* real life is, what the living experience is, and we have no real idea how one might live in such a way as to be in touch with it. That, certainly, is central to our tragic condition.

This, then, is an impossible book: it is a philosophical investigation of something – the tragic nature of life – which resists philosophical comprehension. The gestures towards such a view that it offers are intended to open up space for the reader to think more productively about the issues with which it deals rather than enforce agreement. Of course, I shall be seeking to give reasons for what I think and for the views presented here, but the reader who has followed me this far will know that, in any straightforward sense, I cannot write in the spirit of providing the truth and could not even were it possible to give more than gestures towards the claims this book makes. It would be best if I could write – as Kierkegaard, often seen as the founding father of existentialism, suggested all philosophy should be written – only in the subjunctive. But this, of course, is not possible. In any case, such a reader will also know why it is that I shall be glad if I am able, even if only on occasion, to bear in mind the approach expressed in these comments of Theodor Adorno's:

> Nothing is more unfitting for an intellectual resolved on practising what was earlier called philosophy, than to wish, in discussion, and one might almost say in argumentation, to be right. The very wish to be right, down to its subtlest form of logical reflection, is an expression of the spirit of self-preservation which philosophy is precisely concerned to break down . . . When philosophers, who are well known to have difficulty in keeping silent, engage in conversation, they should always try to lose the argument, but in such a way as to convict their opponent of untruth. The point should not be to have absolutely correct, irrefutable, water-tight cognitions – for they inevitably boil down to tautologies – but insights which cause the question of their justness to judge itself.[23]

ONE

Ontology

In Sophocles' *Oedipus at Colonus* the Chorus, meditating both on the fate of Oedipus and on the nature of the human condition, says at one point:

> Say what you will, the greatest boon is not to be;
> But, life begun, the soonest to end is best,
> And to that bourne from which our way began
> Swiftly return.
> The simple playtime of youth behind,
> What strife is absent, what fierce agony?
> Strife, and the bloody test
> Of battle, envy and hatred.[1]

Sophocles' image could hardly be bleaker: the best thing for us is never to be born, the second best to die soon. It would be hard to think of a more succinct and powerful expression of the sense that life is tragic.

The Chorus seeks to explain its profoundly bleak sense of the tragedy of life by pointing out the ubiquity of suffering in a human life, at least once one is past the 'simple playtime of youth'. Moreover, it is evident that the Chorus thinks of this suffering as something that is not accidental to the human condition. It is, rather, that suffering is central to our very nature, an essential element in what makes us what we are. Part of the Chorus's point is that the young, even if they have to bear suffering and pain, do not yet understand these as essential to human life. And if suffering is central to our existence then this means, among other things, that our suffering bears nothing more than, at best, an arbitrary correlation with our merits or demerits, that its relation with such is not one of justice or logic, but, rather, a question of chance.

Such a view of suffering invites us into the idea that the human condition is tragic because we are not at home in the world. We could put it this way: the tragedy of the human condition is that we are ontologically precarious, and our ontological instability is manifested in, among other things, our suffering. What is meant by this instability is what I seek to explain in this chapter.

You did not choose to be born or where to be born. Nor did you choose your parents or your siblings, if you have any. You did not choose your sex, or your mother tongue or your physical characteristics, and you did not choose the basic features of your character. Nor did you choose the socio-economic class or group into which you were born or the basic opportunities and difficulties that were placed in your way as you grew up. Virtually nothing at the beginning and in the early years of your life was yours to choose. Moreover, throughout life this continues to be so: the people you meet, the interests that you develop, the place you end up living in and much else besides: all of this is largely a matter of luck or chance, good or bad. Further, you have no choice about the fact that the world, your world, is a world which matters to you in various ways, is a world with which, and in which, you are engaged. Something like this was what Heidegger sought to capture by speaking of the way in which we are *thrown* into the world.

Of course, not everyone believes this. Some people believe that it was God's will that they were born and they be as they are. No one can prove that view mistaken, but one might wonder, from the perspective offered in this book, what it conceals, and it would be hard to resist the idea that it masks a thought that is unbearable, namely, just that thought about one's utter contingency. No doubt there are people who are able to look that contingency in the face and not be disturbed by it, but it is also true that it invites one to think of human beings as ontologically unstable, precisely because in being thrown into the world we are thereafter forever seeking to find our feet.

Because we are condemned to spend our life in this search, George Orwell was certainly right when he remarked that 'any life when viewed from the inside is simply a series of defeats.'[2] Or, again, T. S. Eliot has Harcourt-Reilly, one of the characters in his play *The Cocktail Party*, comment that 'the best of a bad job is all any of us make of it,'[3] and that seems to me to capture well the sense not simply that we are forever trying to catch up with ourselves through life, but that what this shows is that there is something fundamentally wrong with human life. Eliot, for example, suggests in the play in question that one manifestation of what is fundamentally wrong is that we cause each other suffering because our relationships with each other are inevitably, and despite the best will in the world, permeated by illusion, illusion from which we can never escape: we can never fully understand what we want of others or what they want of us or why this is so. And this is because we can never understand what we want as such.

If we put together these ideas: that we are thrown into the world, that this requires of us that we make the best of a bad job, and that this reveals something fundamentally wrong with our condition, then we can suggest that for us it is *as if* we had been thrown into existence by beings hostile to us. This sense is, perhaps, most profoundly captured in Gloucester's comment in *King Lear* (Act IV, Scene I) that 'As flies to wanton boys are we to the gods,/ They kill us for their sport'. Nietzsche expresses a similar sentiment in *The Birth of Tragedy*, in which he entertains the thought that there is a capricious child-god who plays with the world by building sandcastles and knocking them down and that our sufferings are merely the by-product of this god's exuberant playfulness. Of course, he does not think that there is such a god, but he does want to suggest that we experience life as if this were so.

It is, perhaps, not surprising that those who look at things this way have a tendency to think that human existence resembles nothing so much as a form of punishment. The attitude in question is well captured by some comments of John Calder's on Samuel Beckett, which bring together much of what I have been saying so far in this chapter:

> What emerges from Beckett's studies of human nature, in the theatre and in his novels [is the view] . . . that man is what he is, each one different, each in his own private hell, living a life trapped in a situation that he did not and could not choose, as good or as bad as his individual nature allows him to be: he is unimprovable and unchangeable in any significant way, trapped as the protagonists of Greek drama were trapped by the gods . . . Beckett believed that the original sin lay in being born at all . . . And life is the punishment for it.[4]

Nietzsche himself resisted the thought that life is a form of punishment, and wanted to be able to see and affirm the tragedy of human life in such a way as to remove from it the sense that life is a kind of penance. But it is far from clear that he was able to do this, not least because there is no doubt that he possessed, or was possessed by, what was in many ways a deeply punitive attitude towards himself. If there was one thing that Nietzsche was not good at, it was being kind to himself, though part of the tragedy of his own life was a deep desire, never satisfied, to learn to do just that.

The fact that Nietzsche was like this and knew himself to be so was one reason why he was fascinated by the ways in which man is so deeply and irremediably at odds with himself. One of the key things he had in mind was that we are each of us caught up in, indeed, each of us *is*, such a tangled and impacted mess of wish, fantasy, hope, longing, fear, anxiety and so on that, in various ways, we often end up sabotaging or hijacking our own deeper purposes and aims – and we may or may not know at the time that we are doing so. Samuel Johnson spoke in this connection of 'the treachery of the human heart' and the phrase is apt: our psychological drives run at such cross-currents to each other that we might think of them as betraying each other – and us.

We can begin to see more clearly what is at stake here by reflecting on the concept of utopia, and one of the most enlightening explorations of utopia is, indeed, to be found in the work of Johnson, in his short novel *The History of Rasselas, Prince of Abissinia*.[5] Rasselas lives in the utopian Happy Valley, where everything he wishes is provided for him. He and his companions, says Johnson,

> lived only to know the soft vicissitudes of pleasure and repose, attended by all that were skilful to delight, and gratified with whatever the senses can enjoy. They wandered in gardens of fragrance, and slept in the fortresses of security. Every art was practised to make them pleased with their own condition. The sages who instructed them told them of nothing but the miseries of publick life, and described all beyond the mountains as regions of calamity, where discord was always racing, and where man preyed upon man.
>
> To heighten their opinion of their own felicity, they were daily entertained with songs, the subject of which was the *happy valley*. Their appetites were excited by frequent enumerations of different enjoyments, and revelry and merriment were the business of every hour, from the dawn of morning to the close of the even.[6]

Rasselas is not, however, able to leave the valley and this is the one thing he comes to long to do. It is, says Johnson, one of the 'wants of him that wants nothing'. The reason he wishes to leave is boredom. As he says to his instructor: 'possessing all that I can want, I find one day and one hour exactly like another, except that the latter is still more tedious than the former.'[7] Rasselas eventually finds a way out of the valley with his sister Nekayah, her attendant Pekuah, and his poet friend Imlac. They search for what Johnson calls 'the choice of life', that is, to find out what is the best and most satisfying way to live. The title of the final chapter is 'The conclusion, in which nothing is concluded', which sums up how far they get.

The key aspect of all this for our purposes is Rasselas's desire to leave the valley; he has everything he wants, but this bores him. Of course, what one might say is that this shows that there is, after all, something he does not have, that there is something he wants. But this is not the point – indeed, it is to miss the point. For what is being shown in Rasselas's predicament is something about the structure of desire: in the valley all his desires are satisfied; there is nothing he wants; yet *he* is not satisfied. There is a gap between one's being satisfied and one's desires being satisfied: to want nothing, to be free of all desires, is to be in a state that resembles nothing so much as a kind of living death which, if sustained, can be nothing but a state of crippling boredom.

The truth is that human beings crave peace, which is what utopia is: a world in which we and all our desires are satisfied, where there is no conflict or suffering or pain. Yet when humans attain this peace they are bored by it. What they need is what one might call an *edge* to life, and they want this even though it is painful, that is, something that cannot exist in utopia. But utopia is supposed to be the perfectly fulfilling condition for human beings. Something has gone badly wrong.

What has gone wrong is that human beings are structured such that two of their fundamental needs or desires – on the one hand, for peace, order, the absence of conflict and the like; on the other, for the kind of forward movement in life that having desire generates – are in conflict with each other. But the point is not simply about desire; it is about our most basic metaphysical relation to the world. For creatures such as we are, there are two conditions that are indispensable, not simply for our well-being but for the very possibility that we can find ourselves at home in the world: security, peace, order, harmony and so on, *and* an absence of these that is disruptive, that stops life collapsing into being nothing more than tedious stagnation. We are in conflict with ourselves at the deepest level because our being-in-the-world is riven by two contradictory trajectories.

In a sense, this dilemma is at the heart of philosophy, and innumerable philosophers have sought to find ways in which to achieve balance between these aspects of the human condition such that one might be not simply not torn to pieces by these conflicting pressures, but actually fulfilled. The problem, however, is much more than that it is difficult to achieve the balance in question. It is rather that human beings are metaphysically in conflict with themselves, that they necessarily cannot have what they are ineluctably called to have, namely, a sense of being at home in the world. In this sense, the human being is an impossibility, what Simon Critchley, in a discussion that parallels mine in certain ways, has called 'an eccentric creature, an oddity in the universe'.[8] Pascal expressed the point by saying that human beings cannot bear themselves. We are, as I expressed it earlier, ontologically unstable or precarious.

One way to put these points would be to say, as Terry Eagleton has said, that 'desire is an anonymous field of force into which we fall as into a sickness, a monstrous fatality or ontological malaise into which we are born and which chooses us far more than we choose it.'[9] We usually think of desire as something we have, something we possess. But, in truth, desire – which includes our longings, needs and the like, that is, conative features of our psychology, but also is, as Eagleton suggests, a basic feature of our ontological condition – is more something that *has us*: we find ourselves in its grip; it works through us and expresses itself in us. We are *possessed by* desire, which leads us out in two opposing directions at the same time: towards order and towards disruption. This is something we are born into and we have no choice but to live with it. The fact that human history is a scene of such monstrous suffering and waste – 'Humanity must perforce prey on itself, / Like monsters of the deep,' says Albany in *King Lear* (Act IV, Scene II) – that history is, as Walter Benjamin said, a permanent state of emergency, is explained at least in part, I think, by the fact that we are ontological misfits and we swing forever between our two opposed metaphysical tendencies. At the individual level this is seen in the fact that all of us, sooner or later, arrive at the point where we realize that through our efforts to achieve some kind of stability our life has become hopelessly compromised: we have hurt others, and been hurt, in irredeemable ways; we are weaker and our lives are more replete with folly than we could ever have imagined; we have wasted time and opportunities; and so on.

I want now to look at three examples, out of the many that one could choose, of the way in which each human being is at odds with himself or herself, since they seem to me especially helpful in helping us to deepen the analysis offered so far and see what is at stake in this issue. The first of these has to do with the struggle human beings have to understand the meaning of what they do and experience. The second and third illuminate crucial aspects of our experience of time, of the fact of our being temporal creatures and that our being so reveals a kind of fundamental ontological precariousness in our existence.

The first example is provided by Gabriel Josipovici in his novel *Contre-Jour*, an imaginary reconstruction of the relationship between the artist Pierre Bonnard and his wife, Marthe, through the eyes of the daughter they never had. The first part of the novel is a long monologue by the daughter, now an adult and living on her own, addressed to the mother. Speaking of a visit she paid to her parents, she says:

> I had no place there. I was only a visitor. Not unwelcome, that would have been too strong. Barely noticed. Hardly there at all. And that was how it had always been. Neither of you really ever knew what to do with me. Your lives were closed to anyone but yourselves. And of course I was never an easy child. Because I felt so completely shut out of both your lives I only clung to you more closely, and this in turn only made you more determined to keep me out, more resolute in your deafness to my appeals.
>
> Perhaps it wasn't really like that though. Perhaps it was always only my fault. Perhaps I merely overreacted to a common complaint, to what they call a fact of life. Perhaps none of it happened as I so vividly remember it, perhaps there never was any sense on your part of wanting to be rid of me, only my inordinate desire for more love than anyone could be expected to give, even to their child, and then my guilt at sensing that I was asking for more than you could give. Or perhaps the guilt had to do with my wanting to escape you both, which I tried to assuage by inventing this story of your rejection of me. I don't know. We act and then we try to interpret those acts, but the interpretations are only further acts, which themselves call out for later interpretation.[10]

The daughter lurches from one interpretation to another, from the sense that now she has found the truth to the sense that what she thought of as the truth is simply something that calls out for further interpretation. What she gradually realizes is that her self-interpretations are limitless and that there is something there that seems to have a life of its own, a kind of psychological reality that seems to resist her struggles to get at what it is. Here truth seems to be at one with falsehood, the struggle for truth feeding from some kind of (self-)deception. We all are like the daughter in this way.

We can, I think, look at the issue in the following way. On the one hand, human beings are capable of understanding and explaining their behaviour in such a way as to make it clear to themselves and others what they are doing, for example, visiting friends or relations, giving a class in philosophy, playing a game and so on. On the other hand, there is another way in which what they are doing remains obscure to them in just the way the daughter in the example shows: they are unable to get clear on the meaning of their actions. What is really going on in this relationship? What does he, does she, do I really want from it? What does it really mean to devote one's life to teaching and writing? Do I really care about being involved in this sport and, if so, why? Is it not, after all, rather pointless? These are exactly the kinds of questions that we can and do ask ourselves as we seek to understand what it is that we are doing with our lives. It is as if we live on two levels: one, at the surface, where we know what we are doing and can explain it, and another, deeper level where we cannot make sense of ourselves. It is no doubt true that we live most of the time on the surface, but there are moments, particularly those of crisis, where we are struck by how little we understand things. Moreover, it also seems to be that a growing sense of our living on the deeper level comes with ageing, as we start to be able to look back across periods of our lives and wonder what they meant – and, therefore, what the present means. This may be one of the reasons why it is said that wisdom or, alternatively, a scepticism about human affairs comes with age.

Human beings are thus at odds with themselves insofar as they are creatures whose actions must appear to them as contradictory: at the one level explicable and comprehensible and at the other obscure and perplexing. It is as if we cannot focus clearly on what we are and it is no doubt because of this that Primo Levi made the point that 'every human action contains a hard core of incomprehensibility'.[11]

The second example I would like to explore is to be found in F. Scott Fitzgerald's novel *The Great Gatsby*.[12] Before the First World War Gatsby loved Daisy but was penniless and could not be accepted in her world of extraordinary privilege ('Her voice is full of money', he remarks at one point).[13] After the war, still impoverished but decorated in military glory, he returns to the United States and in ways that are at least partly highly shady makes a fortune. Daisy, however, has married Tom and has a child, and Gatsby has to wait five years to meet her again. His 'project' during that time, as Sartre might put it, has been to meet her once more and to begin again a life with her which, for him, would mean that all the events of those five years would have been, as he puts it, 'wiped out forever'.[14] His explicitly stated aim is to repeat the past, which means, for him, to restart his life from the point of the beginning of his love for Daisy and change the agony of his loss of her. Hence his friend, who is the narrator of the book, Nick Carraway, says of him:

> He talked a lot about the past, and I gathered that he wanted to recover something, some idea of himself perhaps, that had gone into loving Daisy. His life had been confused and disordered since then, but if he could once return to a certain starting place and go over it all slowly, he could find out what that thing was.[15]

Gatsby's project is profoundly self-thwarting. His deepest need is to change his past because it is unbearable to him, but, in seeking to change it, he acknowledges, however implicitly, the impossible, self-frustrating nature of this project; his project makes sense to him only because the past is the unchangeable thing it is, otherwise he would not be so caught in the toils of seeking to change it. Gatsby wants, finally, to be with Daisy, but he cannot, in fact, bear to be with her except on the condition that his being with her – the future this projects him into – be one that issues from a past other than the one he has had (Nick: "'I wouldn't ask too much of her [Daisy],' I ventured. "You can't repeat the past". "Can't repeat the past?" he cried incredulously. "Why of course you can!"'[16]). He could only bear it if he had had a different past and that is just what he cannot have, so his being with Daisy, the thing he has so longed for, becomes something he cannot bear when he has it. This is why Nick ends the book in this way, reflecting on the green light that had shone out from the end of the quay near to Daisy's house and which had symbolized Daisy's tantalizing proximity to him, and thus the tantalizing proximity of his project's completion:

> Gatsby believed in the green light, the orgastic future that year by year recedes before us. It eluded us then, but that's no matter – tomorrow we will run faster, stretch out our arms farther ... And one fine morning –
> So we beat on, boats against the current, borne back ceaselessly into the past.[17]

What Gatsby shows us, so Nick is saying, is that no life is wholly free from the rush into a future which is, in fact, a fantasy about the past, a desire to make the past something other than it was. The future, he is suggesting, is for human beings always about being carried back somewhere in the past in the hope that the future will be the future of this other, unreal past. This is why Tony Tanner in an excellent essay on the novel, which forms the introduction to one of its editions, ends what he has to say about Gatsby's strange reality that is fake, and falsity that is the truth, by quoting one of the characters in the novel: 'But what do you want? What do you expect?'[18] I take it that his point is that there is nothing else to want and nothing else to expect because Gatsby shows us what we are. From this perspective, one might say that no human being can bear his own past and thus, in this sense, his future. One would need to add, of course, that this feature of the human condition varies a great deal in the way it is manifested psychologically from individual to individual and, moreover, waxes and wanes for any given person.

If Fitzgerald is right, that we can be haunted by our past is but one expression of the fact that there is something about our existence as creatures who have a past that means we cannot be at home in the world. His point, I take it, is, of course, that the past can never be what we want it to be. But this is not, or not only, because it contains or is made up of things that have caused us pain or suffering. It is, rather, simply because of the bare fact that it is past, that is, that time cannot run backwards. This is what Nietzsche called human beings' resentment against time: the fact that we are temporal creatures, aware of our past, is an awareness always of a primordial loss that can never be made good precisely because the past can never be recuperated. It is from here, perhaps, that we get our most profound notion of waste, in a past which, whatever it was, can never return.[19]

We can connect this with the point I made earlier about our basic metaphysical orientation in the world. After all, it might be wondered why it is that the fact that we are temporal beings creates for us the resentment of which Nietzsche speaks, why it is that the past is a scene of loss that can never be made good. And I take it that the reason is that the two trajectories of human existence of which I have spoken – towards order and towards disruption – map onto our temporality. What our forward, temporal projection through life provides is precisely a conception of the disruption of our existence, and it does so for at least two reasons. First, it pushes us towards death, which is the final disruption of everything that a human life is. Second, it leaves behind a past which *fills us up* in the sense that it is the ever-increasing residue of all that we have been and which accordingly is a kind of *primordial inescapable compression* in our experience. That compression is disruption in the form of limitation, pulling us increasingly away from what the world begins by being – or seeming to be – for each of us, namely, a scene of unlimited possibility, precisely a kind of *ordered* world. When Nietzsche speaks of resentment, then, we should not see him as speaking primarily of a psychological state – though, of course, individuals can feel resentment at the passing of time, as Gatsby does – but of a feature of our ontological condition which might be expressed in such a state. He is seeking to display our ontological condition and, indeed, an aspect of our condition that renders it tragic.

Here we can bring in the third example I had in mind: Italo Svevo's novel *La coscienza di Zeno*, the ambiguity of the Italian allowing both *The Conscience of Zeno* and *The Consciousness of Zeno* as translations, although it was, in fact, first rendered into English as *The Confessions of Zeno*.[20] Consideration of this novel will allow us to deepen some of the reflections on time we have been exploring, and then to develop the exploration further.

The central element in Zeno's understanding of himself is the opposition of health and illness. He craves health, which would be, roughly speaking, a kind of full engagement with the world, a capacity to grasp experience as it comes along and be immersed in it, accept it and live in and through it. He does not take this to be the same as being happy or content all the time, but he does take it to be what one might call a kind of transparent relationship between himself and the world, a way in which the world would be open to him and he to the world. But his illness is precisely the incapacity to be like this; somehow he is, indeed, always thwarting his own ends. He resembles nothing so much as the kind of person Baudelaire describes:

> This life is a hospital where each ill person is possessed of the desire to change his bed. One would like to suffer close to the stove, while another thinks he would get better by the window. It always seems to me that I would be fine where I am not, and this question of moving is one that I discuss ceaselessly with my soul.[21]

For example, the book, which is darkly comic, opens with Zeno's pained attempts to give up smoking. He determines to do so again and again, each time smoking 'the last cigarette'. He keeps making resolutions to give up, taking as his cue as a moment to do so some date – the ninth day of the ninth month 1899 or the first day of the first month 1901 and the like – or some event such as his giving up his studies in law to take up chemistry. He even books himself into a clinic to cure himself of his habit, but then spends the whole time there devising stratagems in order to get out before the cure is complete and while he is still longing for a cigarette. What he eventually realizes is that each 'last cigarette' has a special flavour precisely because it is the last. He is deeply emotionally and intellectually invested in something self-refuting – the last which cannot be the last – and he knows it, and also does not know it.

This kind of tangle pursues Zeno throughout his life. Thus, for example, he marries, but determines some time later to take a mistress. Yet his decision is blighted from the first. So, when he meets Carla and decides that she shall be his mistress, he knows already that he will never be able to enjoy her because, as he says, 'My conscience is so delicate that, in the way I went about things, I sought to attenuate the remorse that I would feel in the future.'[22] And again: 'I had already regretted my infidelity so much before committing it that one might have thought it easy to avoid it.'[23]

One of the things that makes Zeno's case so fascinating is not simply that he is self-thwarting, but that he knows he is. Indeed, he knows so clearly that he is that we can see in him an attack on his own capacity to orientate himself towards the good, that is, towards that which he takes to be good in life. He is, in this sense, a kind of self-destructive character, the kind of character who actually wills the destruction of his own aims and purposes and knows that this is what he is doing. But he may not really know, or may only half-know, the reason for his doing this. It is a reason that is almost certainly to be found in the idea of the resentment at the passing of time that I mentioned earlier. What Zeno is doing is crippling his own capacity to form motivations, for example, the motivation to give up smoking, which is why he makes endless and pointless resolutions to do so. And he does this because, whatever else motivations do, they project us into the future. In a sense, what Zeno is doing in seeking to incapacitate his own ability to form motivations is attempting to arrest the flow of time into the future: if his motivations in this way are thwarted, then he does not move into the future – this is the fantasy – and, instead, makes time stop. The primordial resentment of being a creature with a past is then overcome.

Throughout the novel Zeno is in search of individuals he might think of as healthy. His wife, Augusta, is one example, who seems to him, at first, to be the personification of health. One aspect of this is her belief in eternal life, which gives her the confidence that she and Zeno will remain together forever. Further, she is someone who seems at ease in the world. Referring to his own father's horror at the rotation of the planet, Zeno writes of his wife:

She knew all the things that make one desperate, but in her hands these things changed their nature. And if the earth went round it was not necessary to get sea sick! Quite to the contrary! The earth went round, but everything else remained in its place. And these immobile things were terribly important: the wedding ring, all the jewels and clothes – green, black, the walking costume which was put into the cupboard when one arrived at home, and the evening costume which it was quite impossible to wear during the day, and even then only if I put on my tail coat. And meal times were rigidly observed, as well as the times for going to bed. These hours too existed, and they were always to be found in their place.[24]

And so on. Zeno wonders how she can bear the contemplation of pain and death during Mass on Sundays, but 'for her they did not exist, and the visits to church imbued her with serenity for the whole week'.[25] Again, she is reassured by the official structures of the state, who look after public safety, and the presence of doctors, who take care of people's health. Zeno sums it up this way: 'I finally understood what perfect human health is when I grasped that the present for her was a tangible reality in which one could take shelter and keep warm.'[26]

The case of Zeno's wife is deeply instructive. What she has is what Zeno lacks completely: the ability to be at home in the world, to accept the world and things in it for what they are. For her, the present is quite other than it is for Zeno. For him, it is possessed only as the denial of the past and the future, available only as an agonized and agonizing struggle against what was and what is to come; for her, it has none of this, but is welcoming and protective. For Zeno, this is health: above all, no resentment at the passing of time.

And yet there are doubts. Zeno writes:

I am analysing her health, but without much success because I realize that, in analysing it, I convert it into a disease. And, writing about it, I start to wonder whether her health did not need some treatment or training to be cured.[27]

Why should this be? Well, is there not, after all, something unhealthy in taking things at face value as Augusta does? Or, perhaps better, is this the kind of health one really wants? What she seems to lack is a kind of critical insight into things, a capacity to stand back and wonder whether things are really as they seem. Or is she, perhaps, complacent? Might it be that the health Zeno longs for could only be had at the price of complacency? Further, Augusta's health seems to flow partly from her faith, and that expresses a concern that runs throughout this book and which I mentioned at the outset: can one really be at home in the world if one abandons all religious belief? Is not the problem in the modern world, as I suggested, that many can no longer believe in the story that, for example, Christianity tells us? There are, it might be said, plenty of people around who seem to get on with things perfectly well with no Christian faith – that is, they are not troubled by the decay of such faith in the modern world and what it means for our condition. This is true, of course, in one sense. But for Zeno the question is whether one is able to abandon all that goes with such faith and still not see life as tragic. What is it really to abandon such faith and simply accept the world as it is? For Zeno, to do so and really to seek to live without illusion is inevitably to be confronted by the tragedy of the human condition.

At any rate, Zeno raises for us this question: is it possible to be healthy and at the same time fully accept life as it is, without illusion and without self-deception? Could it be that part of what it is for a human being to be healthy is precisely *not* to accept life as it is, to live, at least in part, in an illusion? Is ill-health the price we have to pay for a true grasp on reality?

These questions are at the centre of Nietzsche's thinking, and, roughly speaking, his answer is that those who are most at home in the world, that is, those who are most healthy, are those who fail to see life as it actually is. But then, he adds, even those who seem least healthy have their own forms of illusion, and no one can, in fact, see things as they really are. Man is, for Nietzsche, the sick animal, but that sickness can be a form of health. Gatsby, for example, is sick insofar as he cannot bear his own life in the way we have explored and must live in a fantasy, but that makes him healthy inasmuch as he would not be able to continue living without his fantastical illusions. Human beings, so Nietzsche says, cannot live without illusions, and these illusions are (the expression of) both illness and health. And he thinks, of course, that the most profligate example of this is Christianity: this massive, highly ramified complete explanation of the world is a colossal form of illusion and, in this sense, shows the sickness of those who resort to it; yet it allows those who believe it to live on and make sense of things, which means it provides them with some kind of health.

For Nietzsche, we are deeply and irremediably self-conflicted because not to be so would be to enter into a kind of fullness of life, to be open to life in all its extraordinary multiplicity, and at the same time to see life for what it really is. But that is not possible for human beings, which is why he imagines a creature he calls the *Übermensch*, the Overman, a kind of superhuman creature that man might become. And this is why the notions of life, and the affirmation of life, are at the heart of his thinking, and he conceives such affirmation as, among other things, the capacity to accept the tragedy of life without turning away from it in disgust or horror. This is why he sought to reject the idea that we should see life as a kind of punishment, for that can only be some kind of denial of life. He also thought that to think of life as punishment meant that we would have to ask what we are being punished for. The answer to that could only be that we are punished for being born.

As I said earlier, Nietzsche had a deeply punitive attitude towards himself, and so it is far from clear that he really escaped from the idea of seeing life under the aspect of punishment; maybe his tendency to see things in this way only made him all the more insistent about resisting that outlook. He is surely right that it is possible to see life as tragic without elaborating that in terms of the idea of punishment or original sin. Nonetheless, it is not a surprise that the idea that life is tragic has been articulated in such terms. The imagery is, of course, of Christian provenance, and what it suggests is that the Christian diagnosis of our condition is correct but its redemptive power is exhausted. That is, in its conception of original sin Christianity conceived of human beings as broken and it offered a redemptive vision in which we could be saved through Christ's death on the cross and God's all-embracing love. The tragic view of life, from the present perspective, agrees that there is something fundamentally amiss with human beings, but can no longer accept the redemptive vision; we are left with one key aspect of the Christian story, but that aspect no longer fits into a whole or overall pattern. We are left with the brute fact of our tragic predicament.

Erich Heller wrote of Kafka:

In Kafka we have the modern mind, seemingly self-sufficient, intelligent, skeptical, ironical, splendidly trained for the great game of pretending that the world it comprehends in sterilized sobriety is the only and ultimate real one – yet a mind living in sin with the soul of Abraham. Thus he knows two things at once, and both with equal assurance: that there is no God, and that there must be God.[28]

If, as I have been suggesting, human beings are ontologically precarious creatures, ontological misfits in the world, then for someone like Kafka this tragic view of existence is unbearable without the existence of God to redeem it. What we are left with, rather, is the sense that the only god that exists is one who has, as Tolstoy put it in his *A Confession*, placed us here to play a cruel and mocking joke on us. From this point of view, life is a kind of curse, and that, of course, expresses the opposite of the Christian idea that one ought to think of life as a gift. And to think of life as a curse is, at the very least, to appreciate why Sophocles' Chorus could think that the greatest boon for a human being would be never to be born.

TWO

Pollution

There is no God; there must be God. If that thought is central to our tragic condition then it is borne in upon us all more forcefully in the light of the Holocaust, the Nazis' attempt to exterminate European Jewry, to wipe these people from the face of the earth. Just about everyone is agreed that after Auschwitz things cannot be with same with human beings as they were before. Just about no one is agreed on what that means or how we should understand the change. What I wish to do in this chapter is to suggest one way in which we might understand things here, following the lead of Primo Levi, who survived Auschwitz and spent most of the rest of his life thinking, one way or another, about what it meant, and that of Robert Nozick in a highly stimulating essay on the Holocaust.[1] Levi's suggestion is that after Auschwitz we are tainted and can never again be made clean. I want to try and explore what that means, for the thought is not completely clear, for all its suggestiveness. Implicit in Levi's outlook is the idea that the fact of Auschwitz shows that there is no God, because it is inconceivable that any God could have allowed this to happen – unless he is evil – but the only thing that could clean us would be God's forgiving mercy. This is one way of putting Robert Nozick's point that with Auschwitz the Christian era came to an end and redemption is no longer possible for human beings. From this point of view the Holocaust signals the impossibility of believing in God, yet we have need of God all the more in order to clean, to redeem, us. The event that makes God impossible is the very event from which only God could redeem us.

Of course, I am well aware that there are many who still believe in God. I have no intention here of trying to show that they are mistaken, though I return briefly to the issue at the end of this chapter. I am interested, rather, in trying to see what our tragic condition would look like for someone who accepts what I have said so far about the impossibility of belief in God after Auschwitz.

Nozick, as I have said, has claimed that the Christian era came to an end with the Holocaust. According to Nozick, who writes using a Christian vocabulary though he is not himself a believer, the Holocaust has decisively closed the possibility of any kind of redemption that was offered to us by Christ's death on the cross. This is because, he claims, human beings are now 'desanctified'. By this he means that the extinction of the human race would not be a tragedy as such, even if it would involve innumerable individual tragedies for those who died. It is not, he says, that the human race deserves to be extinguished, but he does think that we have lost our right to continue.

Nozick's line of thought reflects in many ways – seemingly without his knowing it – some comments made by Primo Levi. Speaking in *I sommersi e i salvati* (The Drowned and the Saved) of those who survived as he did, he says:

> The just among us, neither more nor less than in any other group of humans, felt remorse, shame, in short, pain, for the offences that others and not they had committed and in which they felt themselves to be involved, because they felt that what had happened around them, and in their presence, and in them, was irrevocable. It would never again be able to be cleansed; it would prove that man, the human race – we, in short

– are potentially capable of constructing an infinite quantity of pain; and that pain is the only force that can be created from nothing, without expense and without effort.[2]

Like Nozick, Levi sees that human beings are now tainted, sullied; they are, to use an idea that is rarely used these days in this way, polluted. That is an antique ethical notion that was more at home in, for example, ancient Greek thought, and was connected with, among other things, ritual and purification. Levi and Nozick are saying that we now need to be purified; but neither of them thinks this really possible.

What does it mean to say that human beings are now tainted or polluted? And even if those who carried out the atrocities of the Holocaust are tainted, how can we all be tainted by their deeds? It is sometimes said that with the Holocaust a new form of evil entered the world. Yet, when one looks at the extraordinary barbarities of previous centuries, it is hard to make clear why this should be so. As Susan Neiman has commented: 'The claim that Auschwitz represents a form of evil which is radically new persists despite all difficulties in giving reasons for it.'[3]

My own sense is that it might be helpful if we suggest that what the Nazis did was to betray their own humanity. Then we might think that the way in which they did so was so radical that they tainted us all because we share their humanity. From this perspective each of us is a custodian of the humanity in us and we have a duty to safeguard it. On this understanding, the humanity we each have is not, so to speak, ours to do with as we like; we have a duty to care for it, not simply for ourselves but for all of us. That surely captures something powerful in the kind of comments that Levi and Nozick make.

But how, exactly, one might ask, did the Nazis betray their humanity? When Levi said that the Nazis created an infinity of pain from nothing, he spoke of the shame that he and other innocent victims experienced in the face of an offence that had been 'introduced irrevocably into the world of existing things'.[4] It is the phrase 'the world of existing things' that is crucial and carries, I think, the burden of Levi's sense of the Nazis' betrayal of their own humanity. I shall try to say why.

The thought has a haunting quality, and intimates a sense of the preciousness of things and of the way in which the things that exist are non-accidentally related to each other in a web of value so vulnerable and sensitive that violence to or in one part resonates everywhere. This is partly because of the word 'thing', which in its very neutrality, its very capacity to refer to any item in the world, at once removes distinctions between things of different value and yet elevates them all to what might be sensed as a form of seemingly infinite value. The sense of a precious totality is also carried in this phrase by the word 'world', which, in this context, suggests a vision of what there is both infinitely close and attentive to the particularity of all that exists, and yet immeasurably far. And it is *this* sense of things, so I am reading Levi as saying, that the Nazis lacked. They had no sense of the world as a fragile and precious totality, for it was forever subject, for them, to a relentlessly intervening, overweening, hubristic will which was hostile to any manifestation of what simply *is*, to what simply exists in the fullness or completeness of itself, to the *independence* of the world from them. This is why Levi says that the Nazis created an infinity of pain from *nothing*. He means not that they did not have to invest time, energy and resources in creating so much suffering, for they did, but that their doing so was done with no sense of the world as anything other than its being there for their purposes, utterly without its own independent demands. It was, in a sense, nothing to them.

One might also express this by saying that the Nazis had no sense of the sheer being of the world. That may seem obscure, but it is the sense of things that we have when we are struck in wonder, through a particular object, by the sheer fact *that* the world is and that the world is the *way* it is. But no human being, Levi is suggesting, can hear his or her own humanity without at least some moments in which the world appears in this way, in which he or she is struck by the world's being as it is, by its sheer being, by its perfect independence of human will, need, desire, for it is in such moments that one has a just sense of what, Levi intimates, a human being is: a mere fleeting appearance in the face of a world that is magnificently indifferent to our existence, noble in his or her recognition and acceptance of this fact.

There is a sense, then, in which the Nazis were in hell, on at least one plausible understanding of what hell is, and wanted to make sure that everyone else was there too. I mean by this that hell is a condition in which the only thing that matters is the relentless assertion of one's own will, the imposition of what one is upon a world which, from that point of view, is not permitted to make any demands on one and whose resistance is seen as something simply to be negated. No doubt the Nazis did not feel themselves to be in hell. They may have thought themselves to be in heaven. But that is because the feeling of hell in the way I am seeking to capture, in which the world is nothing to the force of the will, is a kind of intoxication. This is what makes it attractive. But this intoxication must, in the end, become stiflingly boring because it cannot engage with an independent world. In this sense, to be in hell, though it might appeal at first, becomes utterly tedious. Yet tedium induces lethargy, the incapacity to change. The Nazis were in hell and could not leave, though they could have. W. H. Auden captures this sense of things very well:

> It is possible that the gates of Hell are always standing wide open. The lost are perfectly free to leave whenever they like, but to do so would mean admitting that the gates were open, that is, that there was another life

outside. This they cannot admit, not because they have any pleasure in their present existence, but because the life outside would be different, and, if they admitted its existence, they would have to lead it. They know this. They know that they are free to leave and they know why they do not. This knowledge is the flame of Hell.[5]

Hell and evil are, from this point of view, boring; but those trapped in hell, consumed by evil, are, indeed, trapped, since they cling to their life because they do not have the energy, that is, the spiritual energy, to change. If they left, they would have to admit not simply, as Auden suggests, that there is another life, but that this life is a life that presents them with a resistance to their will, and it is living with that resistance for which they have no energy, for it is taxing. This is something we all know: we all know in our own lives how tiring the resistance of the world to us can be. The only thing that those in hell can do is to try and get everyone else inside hell with them so that they are not reminded that there is another world outside. Dostoevsky is not the only one, but is perhaps the greatest, to have realized that evil is, in the end, and despite its superficial attractions, unspeakably dull. The evil figure of Svidrigailov in *Crime and Punishment*, for example, acts out of boredom and his evil is that he has no sense of the world as anything other than a site for the exercise of his will. Hence, though he does much to makes others suffer, whether he does good or ill is, to him, in the end, neither here nor there; either way, the world is simply there to be used for his ends.

If what I have suggested captures something of Levi's thinking, then it helps us make sense of his thought that human beings are tainted, polluted by the Holocaust. For we might say that the way in which the Nazis betrayed their humanity was precisely through their refusal, their incapacity, to experience themselves in relation to the world and other human beings as bound to that totality by things not of their own making, and through their resolute attempt to make it impossible for any human beings at all to have a sense of the world as a precious, fragile whole. They sought to remake both their own and all other human beings' relation to the world such that the world could only ever be *nothing* in the sense in which I have been using that idea in this discussion. Such a betrayal would not be, so to speak, simply a betrayal, but a betrayal that sought to make it impossible for human beings even to have the thought that they have, to experience themselves as having, a humanity that they could betray.

This point may seem abstract, but it becomes clearer if we remind ourselves that, at the concrete level, this ambition of the Nazis expressed itself, as Levi says, in the fact that they did all they could to implicate their victims in their own guilt. The most striking and terrible example of this was, as Levi notes, that they constituted groups of prisoners whose job it was to drag out the dead bodies from the gas chambers, extract the gold from the teeth, take the bodies to the crematoria and the like. Those who carried out this work were told when they entered the camp that either they would do this or they would be shot immediately. In this way, as Levi says, their souls were destroyed. He describes it as the most heinous idea the Nazis had. However, since, as not only Levi but also Jean Améry, Hannah Arendt and others emphasize, the camps were the meaning and centre of Nazism, the destruction of the prisoners' souls in this way only expresses in compressed form what their whole way of life was about, namely, as I have suggested, getting everyone into hell with them, changing the kind of creature we are by destroying the possibility of our having a certain kind of relation to the world that is central to defining us as what we are. This was the spirit that animated them; it was what they introduced into the world of existing things.

In a sense, I think we can say that these thoughts help us see why one might want to say that the Nazis sought to be gods, to take God's place in a disenchanted world. 'Will kein Gott auf Erden sein / Sind wir selber Götter', wrote Wilhelm Müller in the cycle of poems *Winterreise*, which Schubert set to music: 'If there is no God on earth / We ourselves are gods'. This is why the Nazis wanted to remake human beings and their relation to the world, why we can say that for them the world was nothing. It is as if they sought to rival God by creating *ex nihilo*. But, as Montaigne pointed out, those who wish to be gods end up as beasts. One is also reminded of Johnson's comment that he who makes a beast of himself gets rid of the pain of being a man. The Nazis' most exhorbitant hubris expressed a hatred of human beings, of the human condition as such. These reflections allow us to say, I think, that if we accept the idea found in the work of Levi and Nozick that we each have a responsibility for humanity, then the Nazis tainted us all.

This view of Levi's – or this view which I have developed from Levi, in the spirit of his writings – expresses a particular ethical perspective, a particular perspective on human beings, on the world and on the relation between them. Someone who rejects it cannot be shown, simply because he or she does so, to be mistaken. Nonetheless, it does seem to express something important about what Levi is getting at in his pained attempts to understand the meaning of what the Holocaust is, and I think that it is independently plausible, certainly worth taking seriously.

Suppose, then, that we accept, even be it only tentatively, this idea that human beings after Auschwitz are polluted, tainted. Nozick expresses this by saying that human beings are now desanctified, by which he means that it would not be a special tragedy if the human species were now ended or obliterated. Does he also mean, as one might suppose, that human beings are no longer sacred, that we should not think of human life as sacred? After all, if human beings are desanctified, this seems to imply that we are each individually desanctified, and, if that is so, it seems that what is being said is that individual human beings are not sacred. I am not sure that Nozick really means this implication. This is in part because Nozick says, as I mentioned earlier, that the end of the human species would involve countless individual tragedies. Further, his sense of the terribleness of what the Nazis did does seem to depend, in fact, in some way, on the idea that human beings are sacred, though I am far from sure that Nozick directly intended that.

It is, of course, very common to hear it said that human beings are sacred. But it is equally common to wonder what that could possibly mean in the absence of a belief in God who made us in his image and who loves us unconditionally – and Nozick does not accept that view. Some say it means nothing at all.

Yet perhaps there is, after all, a sense in which we might think of human beings as sacred even in the absence of God. Perhaps we are baffled by what it could mean to say that human beings are sacred because we want to give positive content to this idea, that is, to say what it consists in. And perhaps that is impossible. But maybe we understand what it means to see human beings as sacred when we see them violated in specific ways.

Here is an example to help make the point more clearly. Alain Resnais' documentary film *Nuit et brouillard* (1955) contains scenes in which we see piles of emaciated corpses, victims of the concentration camps, being bulldozed into common pits; footage of starving prisoners staring listlessly at the camera; images of destitute, desperate people, reduced to a level of hunger, filth and moral vacuity beyond those of one's worst possible imagining. The images are of the kind that keep one awake at night, speechless at the depths of human barbarity. And it is that sense of speechlessness that seems to be crucial. For, so I want to suggest, perhaps it is precisely a sense of the violation of the sacred that leaves us speechless. That is, in watching the film we have the sense not that this is the kind of thing that *ought* not to happen, but, rather, that it *cannot* happen. But it did happen. Hannah Arendt remarked that the Nazis did not show that after the death of God all was permitted; they showed that the impossible was possible. Human beings *cannot* be treated in this way; that lies beyond any possibility for them, any conceivable sense of what they could need, want, deserve, understand, be. Arendt gestured towards this point when she said that it is impossible to find with the Nazis a sense of a fellowship in sin, because what they did exceeds any conceivable development of vice. There was a purity in their evil that defies thought and feeling. And in making the impossible possible, in treating human beings in ways in which they *cannot* be treated, they show us, in negative as it were, what it is to see human beings as sacred. The sense of the impossibility of their being treated in that way, seeing them in that way, carries the sense of their sacredness. But we cannot say in what it is that their sacredness consists. We cannot draw attention to some features of human beings and say, 'This is what makes them sacred.' But we might be able to say, 'The impossibility of their being treated in this way shows them to be sacred.' We know it through its violation, when that impossibility becomes possible.

Yet it is clear that, for all the power of this line of thought, our moral experience here reaches a kind of dead end. I do not mean that it would be appropriate to say blandly that, after all, human beings can be treated as the Nazis treated them – that there is no impossibility here. That would just be a refusal of our perplexity. But the problem is that if we say, as I think we should, that human beings *cannot* be treated as the Nazis treated them, that this is impossible, then this, far from explaining anything, simply expresses our perplexity. It is a valuable and pointful expression, I think, because it captures our sense of total bafflement, but it does not mean that we have understood after all what it might mean to say that human beings are sacred. It is a way of indicating that if we go on saying that human beings are sacred, then we are going round in circles, using a concept whose legitimacy we do not understand.

But suppose that someone now said, noting the confusions into which use of the concept of the sacred leads us, that human beings are *not* sacred. What does that mean? Does it mean that we can do with them what we will? Someone might say that this is absurd; even if human beings are not sacred they have desires and needs, and they can suffer in many ways, and it is on account of all that that we cannot treat them just as we wish. Whether they are sacred is neither here nor there, this line of reflection suggests.

The issue is, however, more complicated. Suppose someone genuinely wanted us to put out his eyes. There are such cases, cases where someone wants some suffering inflicted on him. Suppose, further, that we felt like putting out his eyes. In such a case the person in question can have his desire satisfied and so can we. Still, we might well think that something has gone badly wrong, that it would be an appalling thing to do. The horribleness of the blinding of Gloucester in *King Lear* does not consist simply in the fact that he does not want this; there seems to be a violation here that is much deeper, much more primordial. And, in line with our reflections on the sacred in the context of Auschwitz, we might say that the only way to make sense of this violation is to speak of the sacredness of human life. This, it might be said, is what gives us the very particular horror we feel at the deed. The problem is, however, whether, without the religious backing, we know what we are saying, that is, understand what we are saying, even if we find it the fitting thing to say. What I have been suggesting, in speaking of the impossible made possible, is, of course, that in the absence of such a backing, we do not know what we are saying if we say that human beings are sacred. But neither, we can now add, do we know what we are saying if we deny this, for if we do deny that human beings are sacred we are left with a kind of blank in our moral experience, an incapacity to get at why it is that appealing to needs, desires and the like does not take us close enough to expressing our special horror in the face of the way some human beings have treated each other. The notion of the sacred is one aspect of the Christian world-view that remains with us but of which we cannot make sense if we reject that view.

One might, of course, wonder how it is that the notion of the sacredness of human beings is made any clearer by appealing to the idea that they are made in the image of God who loves them unconditionally. Is that idea not itself baffling? And, if it is, how would it help? Could not a Christian agree that the Nazis treated their victims as human beings cannot be treated? If so, is not the Christian just as baffled by what the Nazis did as are those who cannot accept his view?

I think that the answer is that these are, indeed, mysterious thoughts: we do not know, Christians do not know, what it is to say that we are made in the image of God and that he loves us unconditionally. And Christians, too, can say that what the Nazis did was impossible, but that they did it all the same. Yet the fact remains that what Christianity does is to *place* the sense of mystery. It gives us a reason why it is that the thought that we are made in the image of God and loved by him is mysterious: it locates it in the mystery of God's being and love; it allows us to live with the mystery as part of a structured whole which touches enough points in human life to make the mystery tolerable. Moreover, if the Nazis treated human beings as it is impossible to treat them, as they *cannot* be treated, then the Christian can at least see this as an image of Christ's crucifixion: Jesus too, the Son of God, cannot be flogged, spat upon and crucified; it is impossible to do this to him, but it happened all the same. The mystery of the Nazis' treatment of their victims is located in the mystery of the Passion of Christ and, as such, *placed* in such a way as to enable Christians to live with the bafflement. But for those without such a faith, for whom the idea that human beings are sacred and cannot be treated as the Nazis treated them exists as just a fragment of our cultural inheritance, the mystery is, so to speak, more aggressive: it exists as an idea which survives its context and, lacking this context, must remain all the more baffling.

We have been wondering what it might mean to follow Levi in thinking that human beings are now polluted. The idea of pollution or miasma was for the Greeks profoundly connected with that of ritual: ritual was needed to clean those who were tainted by miasma. It is far from clear that we have, in the modern Western world, the kinds of resources in ritual to carry out the necessary purgation. And if they were available they would inevitably be largely Christian rituals, since we would need something like God's forgiving mercy, expressed through such rituals, to clean us. But that, as I mentioned earlier, is just what we cannot have, because we cannot believe in God after Auschwitz. This is, obviously enough, not the expression of a morally neutral point of view: it is the expression of the idea that we find in, for example, the work of Theodor Adorno – who is famous for saying that poetry after Auschwitz would be a barbarism. Picking up on the idea of the homelessness of modern man, Adorno wrote:

> The destruction of European cities and the concentration camps merely continued the process that the immanent development of technology decided for the houses long ago. 'It is part of my happiness not to be a homeowner,' wrote Nietzsche in *The Gay Science*. One must add today: it is part of morality not to be at home with oneself.[6]

Commenting on this thought of Adorno's, Susan Neiman develops it further:

What remains is only the moral imperative not to deceive ourselves about the magnitude of the modern catastrophe. Decency demands that we refuse to feel at home in any particular structure the world provides to domesticate us. It also requires that we refuse to feel at home in our own skins.[7]

The point here is that, according to Adorno, even if one wanted to believe in God and thought it might be possible, one should reject the temptation, and one should do so on moral grounds. This is not, I think, self-lacerating masochism but rather a sense of what it might be to express solidarity with those whom the evil of Nazism sought to destroy. It is a point of view strangely neglected in contemporary discussion about God: that to believe in God now is indecent.

In a discussion of T. S. Eliot's *Murder in the Cathedral*, Raymond Williams speaks of the play's 'perception of the filth of the beast who is man without God'.[8] That, so the reflections of this chapter suggest, captures something central to our modern tragic condition. It was, of course, Eliot's point.

THREE

Suffering

Whatever else tragedy is about, it has to do with suffering. But those who reflect on tragedy – philosophers, literary critics and others – are in much disagreement about which kinds of suffering are genuinely tragic. After all, it seems right to say that the experience of toothache is not tragic, even though it is, of course, a form of suffering. But then, if not all suffering is tragic, which is?

A traditional answer has been found, not surprisingly, by reflecting on the suffering we see in the tragic theatre. But even here there is disagreement about what it is that makes suffering in the theatre genuinely tragic. Roughly speaking, theorists have tended to suggest that tragic suffering is that of those who are noble, in both the moral and social sense, and who are, for example, exposed to the blind workings of fate, that is, crushed by forces they do not understand, which may be the gods, or exposed by some deep flaw in their own nature, or placed in some crushing dilemma from which there is no escape and in which they must do something terrible. So, for example, Oedipus vows to rid Thebes of the person who is polluting the city, not knowing that it is he himself who has done this – through the workings of fate and chance over which he has no control – by killing his own father and marrying his mother. Or there is Macbeth, the noble and proud warrior, who succumbs to the suggestions of the Weird Sisters and his wife, as they reveal his almost limitless ambition for power and command. And there is Agamemnon, who must sacrifice his daughter, Iphigenia, to the gods so that the wind might blow, allowing the Greek fleet to sail to Troy. He is caught in the conflict between his duty to the Greeks and that to his family, and the tragic dilemma is irresolvable.

Different thinkers see these aspects of tragic suffering in different ways. A. C. Bradley, for example, suggests that the blind workings of fate are not tragic unless they are connected in some way with human agency, that is, unless fate works as it does because it is in some way the expression of that flaw in a person's character that I mentioned previously. So he writes:

> Tragedies which represent man as the mere plaything of chance or a blank fate or a malicious fate, are never really deep . . . But where . . . the impression [is created] that the hero not only invites misfortune by his exceptional daring, but is also, if I may so put it, strangely and terribly unlucky, [then we have what] is in many plays a genuine ingredient in tragic effect . . . It is so even in dramas like Shakespeare's, which exemplify the saying that character is destiny . . . Othello would not have become Iago's victim if his own character had been different; but still, as we say, it is an extraordinary fatality which makes him the companion of the one man in the world who is at once able enough, brave enough, and vile enough to ensnare him.[1]

Bradley also insists that what makes suffering tragic in the theatre is that it is borne nobly and in this way becomes ennobling. George Steiner shares this view, writing that in the tragic theatre 'man is ennobled by the vengeful spite or injustice of the gods. It does not make him innocent, but it hallows him as if he had passed through flame.'[2] Many other thinkers have suggested something similar, namely, that tragic suffering is so because it shows that man is somehow noble in the face of those forces which inflict suffering on him.

Again, it is sometimes suggested that genuinely tragic suffering is that which is irreparable, that is, suffering that cannot be turned to account and from which no good can come. And, of course, the tragic hero might show his nobility of character precisely through his acceptance of such irreparable suffering. Then again, it has been argued that tragedy in the theatre is not just a matter of the tragic hero's being confronted with some terrible ethical dilemma – as, for example, Antigone has to disobey her duty as Creon's subject if she is to honour her dead brother, Polyneices, by burying him – but that the protagonist's suffering is occasioned by committing some kind of defilement or desecration. This links tragedy to religious thought and suggests that in true tragic suffering the gods, or the divine, are always present, and further implies that the tragic hero becomes, through his actions, polluted.

One might also, I think, suggest linking tragic suffering to the notion of evil, since it is certainly true that a suffocating sense of the presence of evil can be characteristic of the tragic theatre. A clear example is *Macbeth*, which presents an almost unrelieved sense of the crushing presence of evil, but others of Shakespeare's plays, such as *King Lear*, suggest something similar, as does, in a different way, Sophocles' *Oedipus the King*.

The difficulty with all these views is that it is not so hard to find cases of genuinely tragic suffering that do not fit them neatly. For example, Steiner certainly thinks that Shakespeare's *Timon of Athens* is a tragedy, but Timon is not ennobled by his suffering: he turns from being someone who gives away money in a profligate manner to someone who gives nothing but invective to his so-called friends who let him down when he needs their help – 'Timon is a pathological giver'[3] commented W. H. Auden – and he dies alone and miserable. And if achieving some nobility of soul has something to do with learning, learning of the kind, that is, that we think of as wisdom, then Timon does not seem to learn much. That is why Auden makes the point that Timon goes on giving: at root, he is just doing the same thing all the time, precisely because he learns nothing. Indeed, Auden remarks that 'the big figures in Shakespeare's tragedies do not learn anything – that is the ultimate tragedy of Shakespearean tragedy.'[4] The point is contentious, but one sees what he means. Or again, the idea that tragic suffering is irreparable does not seem quite right: Macbeth's suffering is tragic, as is the suffering he unleashes on Scotland and its inhabitants, but order is eventually restored and new meanings created from the wreckage. Similarly, Aeschylus' trilogy *The Oresteia* ends in resolution, but is considered one of the greatest tragedies of Western theatre. Steiner, who insists that 'tragedies end badly', has to confront this fact about not only *The Oresteia* but also *Oedipus at Colonus*. He writes:

> Not that Greek tragedy is wholly without redemption. In the *Eumenides* [the last play of *The Oresteia*] and in *Oedipus at Colonus*, the tragic action closes on a note of grace. Much has been made of this fact. But we should, I think, interpret it with extreme caution. Both cases are exceptional; there is an element of ritual pageant commemorating special aspects of the sanctity of Athens. Moreover, the part of music in Greek tragedy is irrevocably lost to us, and I suspect that the use of music may have given to the endings of these two plays a solemn distinctness, setting the final moments at some distance from the terrors which went before.[5]

But this argument is very strange. It amounts to saying that we should not take seriously the element of redemption for and in the tragic action, which means that Steiner is insistent on preserving his thesis at all costs. He has, after all, as he admits, nothing more to go on than a suspicion.

Again, it is not even clear that the tragic hero needs to be anything like that which he is traditionally conceived to be, namely, someone of high rank in the social world. Büchner's Woyzeck in his eponymously named play suffers a genuinely tragic fate, but is a downtrodden soldier, right at the bottom of the social pile. Or again, Strindberg's *Miss Julie* is surely a tragedy, but it is hard to see that notions of pollution, defilement and desecration are the key to understanding the tragic situation presented; power seems much closer to the centre. And the gods are nowhere to be seen. As for evil, it seems that not all tragedies present such a sense. Büchner's *Danton's Death* is a great political tragedy, but the play's sense of tragedy comes less through the presence of evil and more through a sense of the futility and pointlessness of human endeavour and aspiration, of waste and absurdity.

Part of what most of those who think about the suffering of the tragic theatre are interested in is the idea that there is some kind of affirmation to be had from watching a tragic play – though Steiner for one, consistently with his claim that tragedy precludes redemption, seems to deny that there is such an affirmation, and hence ends up saying that most of those plays thought to be tragedies, such as *Macbeth*, turn out not to be tragedies after all.[6] For indeed, it seems that only if there is some kind of affirmation to be had in watching a tragedy would it make sense for us to do so. Otherwise, why expose ourselves to the sight of pain, suffering, waste and destruction? Various answers have been proposed to this question, and the idea that the tragic theatre gives us some kind of insight into the reality of our condition seems in many ways the most plausible. On this view, in the tragic theatre we are able to face, as we would not in reality, the fact that human life is, indeed, a scene of suffering and destruction, and that the human heart is full of extraordinarily dark fantasies and longings – which, for moral reasons, we keep well covered in everyday life. Moreover, part of what seems to be at issue here is *the way in which* suffering is expressed in the tragic theatre. That would mean that central here is the language of the play. What I am suggesting, as others have suggested, is that often, if not always, the language in which tragic heroes express themselves is itself noble or elegant or the like, and it is this quality of language that is central to the affirmative nature of suffering in the tragic theatre.

This brings us up against suffering outside the theatre, in everyday life, and its relation to suffering in the theatre. For what I am suggesting is that the tragic theatre can create a kind of illusion about suffering, lending to it a quality that it would not otherwise have. For even if suffering in the tragic theatre readily seems to us affirmative in some way, in reality, to suffer, as such, is not to submit to something noble, although, of course, someone may react to his suffering in a noble manner. Dostoevsky said that the only thing he really feared was not to be worthy of his suffering. That is a deeply noble attitude. But suffering is sometimes, perhaps often or even always, simply banal or squalid or futile or just plain awful – or otherwise not noble, even if the sufferer's reaction to it is. Of course, I do not doubt that suffering can (sometimes) ennoble someone or deepen his view on life or make him wise – though it can also make him bitter, resentful and angry – but, as I have already said, this is not, I think, special to the tragic theatre: it sometimes happens there, and it sometimes happens in real life. The theatre (usually) has the advantage of magnificent language; yet that is not the same thing as the capacity of suffering to be ennobling.

This point is brought out well and in a deliberately irreverent manner in a short poem by D. H. Lawrence:

When I Read Shakespeare

When I read Shakespeare I am struck with wonder
that such trivial people should muse and thunder
in such lovely language.

Lear, the old buffer, you wonder his daughters
Didn't treat him rougher,
the old chough, the old chuffer!

And Hamlet, how boring, how boring to live with,
so mean and self-conscious, blowing and snoring
his wonderful speeches, full of other folks' whoring!

And Macbeth and his Lady, who should have been
    choring,
such suburban ambition, so messily goring
old Duncan with daggers!

How boring, how small Shakespeare's people are!
Yet the language so lovely! like the dyes from gas-tar.[7]

Lawrence's attitude towards Shakespeare's characters may not be entirely fair, but he brings out well the sense that even banal suffering can be made magnificent through the poet's use of language. Nietzsche made a similar point in *The Gay Science*:

The Greeks (or at least the Athenians) liked to hear good talking: indeed, they had a hungry longing for it, which, more than anything else, distinguishes them from non-Greeks. And so they demanded good talking even from passion on the stage, and revelled in the unnaturalness of dramatic verse with delight – in nature, passion is just so sparing of words! so dumb and awkward! Or, if it finds words, so confused and un-reasonable and ashamed of itself! We have now, all of us, thanks to the Greeks, become accustomed to this unnaturalness on the stage, just as we endure, indeed willingly endure, that other unnaturalness, passion that sings, thanks to the Italians. It has become a need of ours, which we cannot satisfy from the resources of actuality: to hear people talk well and with clarity in the most trying situations: by now it delights us when the tragic hero still finds words, reasons, eloquent gestures, and in the whole a bright spirituality where life approaches the abysses, and where in reality a person mostly loses his head, and certainly his fine language. This kind of *deviation from nature* is perhaps the most agreeable nourishment for man's pride: he loves art as such on account of it, as the expression of high, heroic unnaturalness and convention.[8]

So I am suggesting that the theatre can create an illusion about the nature and value of suffering. Moreover, one should not forget that attention to the sufferings of the tragic hero in the theatre is in many ways much easier than is attention to the plight of those who suffer in real life. For one thing, it does not demand anything of us, as real suffering might do, which calls us to alleviate it or live with a bad conscience – or ignore it in order to avoid the bad conscience. For another, the suffer-ing of others in real life can sometimes threaten us too, and this makes it a hard sight to bear.

This is important because it is sometimes said that suffering outside the tragic theatre is not tragic. As Steiner has it: 'The tragic personage is nobler and closer to the dark springs of life than the average human being.'[9] Thus, for example, although we regularly refer to a child's being knocked down by a car, or an industrial accident or the cap-sizing of a boat with great loss of life as tragic, philosophers and literary critics often deny that we should think of these things as tragedies. They do not, after all, usually involve the kinds of things we have been looking at from the tragic theatre: the fate of a people or nation does not hang on such events, as they do on Oedipus or Macbeth or Agamemnon, and we are not (usually) dealing with especially noble characters or individuals cursed by some deep and tragic flaw in their character. So, even if we are unclear about the nature of suffering in the tragic theatre, as I have been suggesting we are, we might still insist, as Steiner does, that, whatever such suffering is, it is not like the suffering of ordinary life, which we should not, accordingly, think of as tragic. Should we say, then, that these forms of suffering are not, after all, tragic?

Those who say not usually add that the modern age is inhospitable to tragedy because we no longer believe in the blind workings of fate and the like: we believe in progress and reason, we are optimistic, we think nature can be harnessed and controlled, and so we have no conceptual and spiritual space left for the tragic. When we use the term with respect to ordinary forms of suffering of the kind mentioned, so these thinkers add, we should not really do so: we are availing ourselves of a debased form of reflection, a debased vocabulary, and we ought to resist this. Moreover, it might be added, under such cultural conditions, the creation of tragic plays for the theatre is well nigh impossible: we just do not have the spiritual and cultural resources to create in this way. This is Steiner's view.

I am not so sure. As I have suggested, there seems to be something mistaken in insisting that ordinary suffering is not tragic because it is not like the suffering in the tragic theatre, since central to the difference is the language in which the suffering is expressed, and, in the midst of dreadful suffering in real life, there is little spiritual space for the kind of magnificent expression that we can often find in the theatre. When one is suffering, one is trying to cope, and that takes up pretty much all of one's energy. Moreover, what controls our response to the tragic theatre is the mastery of the playwright, who crafts something that is, in various ways, intellectually and emotionally enthralling and captures our attention, indeed captivates us. Of course, we could just say that it is the language and the rest that make the difference and leave it at that: suffering outside the theatre is not tragic, but it is no less the significant for all that. But what this misses is that people sometimes do react with nobility to their suffering in real life. There is no doubt, for example, that if we consider, say, Primo Levi's first book about his time in Auschwitz-Buna, *If This is a Man*, then we see that he bore his suffering with a dignity that would be beyond most of us. Indeed, all his writings show his extraordinary courage, sober-headed reflection and nobility of soul. Of course, I am assuming that we can infer from his writings to his life, and this is always contentious, for reasons that I articulated in the Introduction; I am sure that he did not display the same dignity we see in his books all the time in his everyday life, since life is simply not like that. Nonetheless, his writings certainly reveal an attitude towards his suffering which, even if it was his only on occasion, would be extraordinary. It would be silly, after all, to insist that only those who are noble all the time are really noble; even the best can be shallow and foolish at times.

Should we say it is the quality of Levi's reaction to his suffering that makes it tragic? Perhaps, though many would surely want to say that all those in the camps were subject to their own individual tragedies, even if they did not bear their suffering as Levi bore his. Perhaps one might even suggest that those who were ground up by the death camps without having the opportunity or capacity to bear nobly what they underwent suffered an even greater tragedy than those like Levi. Although he does not use the word, he seems himself to imply this, since he insists that those who survived did so through luck and a relentless concern for themselves which closed them to the needs of their fellow prisoners. The best died, and they are the ones who should have testified. And we are still confronted by the case of the child run over by a car or the industrial accident, and these seem to many to be tragic, even if thinkers such as Steiner would disagree.

I do not think that there can be any clearly defined or principled way in which to say that some suffering is tragic and some not. Everything will depend on the details of the case. The situation here is no different from that with many other concepts, and the key issue is to use the term responsibly. The term 'evil', for example, is often used irresponsibly in political discourse, simply as a way of demonizing one's enemies. But that does not mean that we can find some essence of that which is evil or some definition of the term such that we can say which deeds or situations or persons are evil, the rest being something else – brutal or cruel, say, but not evil. Nor does it mean we should avoid the term at all. It just means we should try to think carefully what we are saying when we do use it. So it is with the term 'tragedy' when we use it of suffering. Toothache, as I said, is not tragic, and when the president of FIFA, Sepp Blatter, claimed, referring to the practice of deciding drawn football matches by a penalty shoot-out, that such a way of coming to a result was tragic – 'Football can be a tragedy when you go to penalty kicks' – we know that we are not dealing with a very thoughtful use of the term, though the president's comments are, of course, unintentionally funny, a kind of buffoonery. But plenty of ordinary suffering is, I think, rightly thought of as tragic.

Nonetheless, some ordinary suffering, that is, suffering outside the theatre, that we might be tempted to think of as tragic is not so, in my view. I suppose that we have a strong tendency to suppose that, in saying that some suffering is tragic, we are expressing a sense of its *absolute* terribleness, as if we were saying the strongest or the most powerful thing about it that we can. But I am not sure that we should think this. It seems to me that there are some forms of ordinary suffering whose quality of awfulness is so deep that to speak of a tragedy in such a context is to dignify something that, in fact, renders us speechless. For example, in 1971 Werner Herzog made a film entitled *Land des Schweigens und der Dunkelheit* (Land of Silence and Darkness), which explores the life of Fini Straubinger, a woman who has been deaf and blind since adolescence, and at the same time reflects upon the condition of several individuals who, unlike Straubinger, were born deaf and blind. For our purposes, what emerges from the film, and despite the extraordinary work of those who care for such persons, is the sense of absolute, unmitigated terribleness of the fate of those who have never known what it is to see colour and light, and who have never heard any sound – birdsong, the human voice, music. I am not sure how one might describe their suffering, but, whatever else one might say, to think of it as tragic would seem to me to be wholly inadequate. I suppose one might have the sense that it is as if the suffering of each of these individuals expresses in a way the whole of the world's suffering, as if *there* we see the absolute fragility and vulnerability of the human being, of our transience and pain. But I do not want to insist on that; I simply want to say that the notion of the tragic seems to me in such cases to be itself too banal to be appropriate.

So, I want to suggest, some everyday suffering is tragic and some not. It will all depend, as I say, on the situation. An idea from the work of Wittgenstein is helpful here. In a discussion of games, he asked what it is that all games have in common. After all, cricket, football, ring-a-ring-a-roses, chess, back-gammon and so on are all games, yet they seem to be in many ways very dissimilar. Wittgenstein suggested that they possess what he called family resemblances. They are, he proposed, similar in the way members of a family might be similar – this or that facial feature, sense of humour, accent, manner of walking and so on – even though they might differ from each other in many other ways and even though it might be in some ways or in some contexts difficult to see that they are, indeed, members of the same family. Likewise, we could say, what makes one form of suffering tragic is its family resemblance to some other form of suffering, even if there are otherwise many differences between them.

Consider, for example, the kind of suffering Simone Weil referred to as 'affliction' (*malheur*). She described this as a form of suffering which involved psychological, physical and social elements: deep mental and physical pain in such a case is allied to the sufferer's sense of being a social outcast to such a degree that he might feel himself, quite erroneously, to be responsible for his own suffering. His suffering turns back on itself, and he lacerates himself in his own agony. It is highly plausible to think of this suffering as tragic, partly because it is so intense and deep, and partly because it involves this terrible aspect of the victim's own self-condemnation. But, of course, not all suffering is like this, though some forms of suffering may bear a family resemblance to it. And it has to be added that it is precisely not the kind of tragic suffering with which we are confronted in the tragic theatre. Indeed, Weil formulated her conception of *malheur* while working among factory workers, and these are just the kind of ordinary people about whose suffering the tragic theatre is largely silent. They certainly seem, however, to be close to what Steiner called 'the dark springs of life'. That is part of Weil's point.

In fact, one of the things that seems odd in the denial that there is tragic suffering in real life, including, or especially, real modern life – that is, in those parts of the developed world that many of us are so lucky to live in – is that, despite the extraordinary prosperity by which we are surrounded, and from which we benefit, we are in many ways the victims of bureaucratic, economic and political forces we do not understand and over which we have precious little control. Further, our technological progress might at any moment turn on us and destroy us, and it is becoming increasingly likely that we are racing towards an ecological disaster whose dimensions we can hardly fathom. And beyond that, we live in a world of war, genocide, famine and disease, and part of the tragedy is that those of us who are lucky enough not to have to face these things in our own daily lives contribute to them all the time, partly through indifference and partly through our being caught up in those economic and political structures to which I have referred and which disable us from doing much to help when we do care. The tragedy of those who suffer from our indifference is almost certainly unimaginable to most of us because it is so unimaginably awful.

There is, further, a sense in which ordinary suffering is, or can be, so tragic precisely because it can be so banal. Consider in this context some comments of Auden's on Shakespeare's *Antony and Cleopatra*. He is referring to the theory of the 'tragic flaw' in the hero of the tragic theatre:

> The nature of the tragic flaw in *Antony and Cleopatra* . . . is not of the ordinary specific kind, but this makes for the tremendous power of the play. We see malice and ambition in Richard III, ignorance in Romeo and Juliet, melancholy in Hamlet, ambition in Macbeth, paternalism and the demand for love in Lear, pride in Coriolanus, the desire to be loved in Timon, and jealousy in Othello. These are states of pure being that have a certain amount of police court cases or psychiatric clinics in them, but we are not likely to imitate them. We may feel as they do on occasion, but these people are really rather silly. We wouldn't murder a guest at a party, nor are we likely to run out of the house in the middle of a storm. We think people are crazy to behave like that. We read about such behavior in the papers. Antony and Cleopatra's flaw, however, is general and common to all of us all of the time: *worldliness* –

the love of pleasure, success, art, ourselves, and con-
versely, the fear of boredom, failure, being ridiculous,
being on the wrong side, dying. If Antony and Cleopatra
have a more tragic fate than we do, that is because they
are far more successful than we are, not because they
are essentially different . . . We all reach a time when
the god Hercules leaves us. Every day we can get an
obsession about people we don't like but for various
reasons can't leave. We all know about intrigues in
offices, museums, literary life. Finally, we all grow old
and die. The tragedy is not that this happens, but that
we do not accept it.[10]

Auden is insisting that ordinary suffering can be tragic –
I have been suggesting the same thing, of course – and his
reason for doing so is that such suffering is revelatory of,
manifests, the tragedy of the human condition. And central
to that – Auden would agree – is just what the *Book of
Common Prayer* says:

Man that is born of a woman hath but a short time to
live, and is full of misery. He cometh up, and is cut
down, like a flower; he fleeth as it were a shadow, and
never continueth in one stay.
    In the midst of life we are in death . . .

Man is born to suffer. I have already suggested why this is
so when I spoke in Chapter One of the way in which human
beings are so deeply at odds with themselves. And it is because
this is so that it is in suffering that human reality most deeply
reveals itself.
    But now we might wonder if this is so. In his wonderful
book *The Varieties of Religious Experience* William James drew
a distinction between what he called 'the healthy soul' and
'the sick soul'. He describes the healthy soul thus:

In many persons, happiness is congenital and irre-claimable. 'Cosmic emotion' inevitably takes in them the form of enthusiasm and freedom. I speak not only of those who are animally happy. I mean those who, when unhappiness is offered or proposed to them, positively refuse to feel it, as if it were something mean and wrong. We find such persons in every age, passionately flinging themselves upon their sense of the goodness of life, in spite of the hardships of their own condition.[11]

The outlook of the healthy soul, he says, involves 'a way of deliberately minimizing evil', whereas the sick soul has

a radically opposite view, a way of maximizing evil, if you please so to call it, based on the persuasion that the evil aspects of life are of its very essence, and that the world's meaning most comes home to us when we lay them most to heart.[12]

Is the claim that I have made, namely that the tragic condition of man is that he is born to suffer, not, after all, one might wonder, an expression of a sick soul? And, if it is, where does this leave things from the point of view of the tragedy of life?

James is surely right: there simply are people to whom the idea that life is tragic (for the kind of reasons I have been giving) is alien. I said as much at the outset of this book in suggesting that what I intended to offer here was one possible view on life, a view for which one can give reasons and which seems to me to tell the truth about our condition but which cannot, nonetheless, claim to be *the* truth about the human condition. And I say this despite the fact that James, in a quite brilliant passage, goes on to claim that the view of the sick soul triumphs, in the end, over that of the healthy soul. To the sick soul, he says, healthy-mindedness pure and simple seems unspeakably blind and shallow. To the healthy-minded way, on the other hand, the way of the sick soul seems unmanly and diseased.

[Yet] it seems to me that we are bound to say that morbid-mindedness ranges over the wider scale of experience, and that its survey is the one that overlaps. The method of averting one's attention from evil, and living simply in the light of the good is splendid as long as it will work. It will work with many persons; it will work far more generally than most of us are ready to suppose . . . But it breaks down impotently as soon as melancholy comes . . .

The normal process of life contains moments as bad as any of those which insane melancholy is filled with, moments in which radical evil gets its innings and takes its solid turn. The lunatic's visions of horror are all drawn from the material of daily fact. Our civilization is founded on the shambles, and every individual existence goes out in a lonely spasm of helpless agony. If you protest, my friend, wait till you arrive there yourself![13]

As I mentioned earlier in this book, I think that the key here is to resist, so far as one can, the temptation to turn the tragic view of life into something of which one wishes to convince others. The problematic is clearest in the work of Emil Cioran, to whom I referred at that point. Again and again he traces the ways in which man is the dogmatic animal who is forever turning his ideas into something that everyone else should believe, forever seeking to propose that all the others should believe what he believes. Not only is this, suggests Cioran, politically and morally disreputable and dangerous, it is also, he thinks, intellectually bankrupt, the expression of an elevation of the personal into the impersonal, the local into the metaphysical. Yet it is inescapable: even sceptics, he says, try to convince others of their scepticism. The tragedy of our condition follows us everywhere even as we try to shake it off: at every turn we are bent back against ourselves and we consume ourselves in the attempts to consume nothing, scepticism turning into dogmatism and exhausting itself in its own self-contradictions.

At any rate, Cioran would certainly have agreed with a claim central to Nietzsche's thinking that what we fear more than suffering is *meaningless* suffering. Levi brings out extraordinarily clearly this need we have to find meaning in suffering when he draws our attention to the ways in which the Nazis managed to make the suffering of the concentration camps meaningless for their victims. The key example, emblematic of so much that Levi reports of the camps, is the moment in which, newly arrived in the camp and desperately thirsty, he broke off an icicle in order to quench his thirst. Suddenly he felt a brutal jab in the back. 'Why?' he asked. '*Hier ist kein Warum*' – 'Here there is no why' – came the response. The Nazis knew perfectly well that to instil in their victims a sense of the absolute pointlessness of their suffering was the supreme way of giving that suffering the destructive effect they desired. Levi again and again makes clear that those who believed in anything – it did not matter what – and were therefore able to put their suffering into a narrative which made sense of it, gave it a meaning, were better equipped to survive. What the human mind craves is a reason for suffering. If it finds one, this does not make it go away, but it does, in a way, do something, often a great deal, to make it bearable.

Christianity is, among other things, a massive system for making sense of suffering. Its central image, that of Christ on the cross, is crucial here. Weil, for example, says that even affliction is one of the deepest ways in which we can come close to God, since we have the image of Christ's suffering on the cross as the deepest form of affliction. More generally, Christianity interprets suffering in many ways: as a punishment, as a test, as necessary for moral growth. And it tells us also that, in the end, there is no unjust or pointless suffering, since those whose suffering is pointless here below will find later that it makes sense after all. It is no doubt awful for the sinners who are punished in an afterlife, but at any rate their suffering makes sense.

What Christianity offers is redemption. But this redemption is quite different from the kind of affirmation that may be offered in the tragic theatre. This is because even those tragedies that end in affirmation offer it, so it seems, in general terms: *Macbeth* suggests redemption for Scotland, and Macbeth's own suffering, as well as that of his wife, of Duncan, of Banquo and so on. All can make sense in terms of the narrative of bringing good out of evil, but what the play does not do is suggest that the suffering of each of these individuals makes sense *for* him or her, that is, subjectively, in his or her life as experienced. For example, Banquo's bloody murder is part of the narrative that ends in affirmation, and to that extent makes sense, but it has no meaning *for Banquo*: he is simply brutally murdered, his life is cut short and *for him* there is no meaning in his suffering. Christian redemption, on the other hand, is a redemption not simply *of* each person but *for* each person: it claims that suffering will make sense to each individual in the interiority of his own subjectivity. If there is redemption in the tragic theatre for the characters in a play, then it is very distant from the redemption that Christianity offers. And if there is some kind of tragic affirmation in the theatre for the spectators, as I suggested earlier, then this is even further removed from any kind of Christian affirmation of suffering. The best we are likely to get in that respect in the tragic theatre is a sense that we can look a little more clear-sightedly and honestly at human life as a scene of suffering. Christianity offers something much more ambitious: 'And God shall wipe away all tears from their eyes; and there shall be no more death, neither sorrow, nor crying, neither shall there be any more pain: for the former things are passed away' (Revelation 21:4).

FOUR

Virtue, Happiness and Morality

Throughout almost the entire history of Western thought, philosophy has been haunted by the idea that the person who is morally good might be some kind of fool or dupe. The central reason for this is that it is clear that morality is in many ways largely about various forms of renunciation: to be just to others, to take into account others' needs and desires, clearly requires that one forego things for oneself. This is why moral injunctions are so often framed in terms of what one must or ought *not* to do: steal, lie, cheat, kill and so on. Examples abound. Here are three or four that happen to come to mind.

In Pedro Almodóvar's film *Tacones lejanos* (1991), released in English as *High Heels*, Becky del Páramo, a famous singer, vain and egotistical, abandons her daughter, Rebeca, to the child's father so that she can pursue her career. But the decent thing for her to have done would have been to renounce or limit her career to care for her daughter, as she well knows, and at the end of the film she finally acknowledges this, seeking forgiveness from her daughter. Or there is Frank Troy in Thomas Hardy's *Far from the Madding Crowd*, who carries for Bathsheba Everdene the intoxicating appeal of a roving sexual energy edged with violence, which he uses to manipulate her in an expression of his own lust, desire to dominate and need to impress. Only by renouncing his own needs would he have been able to do what morality evidently required of him. Or again, in Conrad's *Lord Jim*, Jim's jump from the damaged ship, which was on the point of sinking, or so it seemed, leaving the pilgrims to their fate, was certainly cowardly. The courageous thing to do, namely, remain on the ship, might well have required him to sacrifice his life – which is precisely why he jumped. Finally, to offer one more example, Jean Genet in his *Journal du voleur* (Thief's Journal) describes his early life of theft in ritualistic terms, lending to the life of the thief an almost mythic status. Yet clearly morality would have required of him that he renounce all that strange and beguiling poetic pleasure.

The fact is, morality commands us and fills our lives with obligations. It is *hard*. Why should I be moral? is a question that all of us will face, sooner or later, implicitly or explicitly.[1]

It is obvious that those who go through life with less or little regard for moral demands can, in many ways, enjoy things that those who are encumbered by a moral conscience cannot, precisely because they do not experience the need to forego things in the way that the latter do. Their path through life is in some ways easier since morality places restrictions in our way, burdens us with demands. Speaking to an architect recently, I heard how, on two or three occasions during his career, he had been contracted to do work for clients who, when the work was finished, simply did not pay up. It would have been far too costly and distressing to pursue these clients through the courts, so the architect simply wrote off his losses, but was left, of course, with a feeling of anger and bitterness. But the clients got the work done and kept their money. In one clear and obvious sense, they were better off for being unscrupulous since, had they been otherwise, they would have paid and ended up with less. The good person who could never have done that, or who would have suffered from a ter-rible conscience had he not paid, is clearly worse off in some way. Of course, he is morally better; about that there is no doubt. But, one might ask, is it better to be morally upright or is that just a form of foolishness or gullibility? Is morality not in this sense some kind of a 'fraud', as the philosopher Philippa Foot puts it?[2]

It is of course true that, for the person who cares about morality, things are more complicated. The decent person who does not pay his architect will suffer from the sting of his conscience and, in that sense, will in one way be badly off. That is just a way of saying, more generally, that the person who cares about morality will find his good partly in such caring. If someone cares about virtue – as many philosophers tend to put the thought these days – then that caring will be part of his good and he will benefit from being morally decent. Moreover, it is true that human beings in some ways need the virtues 'as bees need their stings', as the philosopher Peter Geach puts it.[3] Someone totally devoid of courage, for example, would not get far in life since at least a modicum of courage is required to do many things in life, from crossing the road in heavy traffic to taking on a new and worthwhile but difficult job. Still the fact remains that, as one might say, only the good person can suffer from a bad conscience. Of course you might say that the perfectly good person will not suffer from a bad conscience, since, in being perfectly good, he will do nothing wrong and thus not suffer in this way. But this is, surely, to abuse our notion of what we mean by a good person. Apart from the fact that there is no perfectly good person and could not be, it is also true that the good person can, and no doubt will, do much that is morally suspect. One of the things that Shakespeare was exploring in the figure of Macbeth, for example, was the case of a good man who does evil. To insist that Macbeth cannot be a good man because he does evil would be to miss the point of the play entirely.

The fact remains that morality involves renunciation, even if it is true that being morally good forms part of the well-being of the decent person. That is why philosophers have been haunted by the idea that the morally good person might be some kind of fool. If morality involves renunciation, then why care about it at all? If someone who does not care about morality is likely, for that very reason, to be able to get more of the good things in life, to find life less encumbered with demands, than the person who does care, then it seems that the morally good person really is some kind of fool.

For this reason countless philosophers have sought to show that being morally good is more important than other things, such as having one's cake and eating it, as in the case of the architect's dishonest clients. What stops the honest client from being a fool, it is claimed, is that, in being honest, he is, after all, better off than the dishonest client with his redesigned house and his money. It is more important to be honest, so the thought goes. Appearances are misleading: it *seems* that morality is about renunciation, but it is not, because, looked at correctly, it turns out that being morally good is a form of obtaining – is, indeed, the central way of obtaining – something that we all want.

That is a way of saying that the importance of morality has to be something that shows up in the life of the good person, something that the good person possesses that the bad person does not. And it cannot show up simply as his being honest, since the dishonest person will just say: 'For sure, he is honest; but he is a fool nevertheless, because his honesty stops him from getting some good things, complicates and burdens his life.' It shows nothing, after all, to say that the honest person is better off being honest because he cares about being honest. We know that. The issue is: why should he care about being honest at all?

Philosophers who have sought to answer that question have therefore often attempted to show that there is some kind of reason to care about being honest – and, more generally, being morally good – that could show that the morally disreputable person is missing something crucial about what makes for a good life. Some have tried to show that that thing is rationality, in the sense that it is irrational to be wicked: if being morally disreputable is irrational, so the thought goes, then the wicked person is the victim of something from which the good person is free, namely, irrationality. On this view, the wicked person is in a mess because he lives irrationally, while the good person lives rationally and thus better than the wicked. Others have resorted to the idea that God will reward the good and punish the wicked, so the good are, after all, better off. Still others have claimed that the reason to be morally good lies in the idea that being such contributes to peaceful cooperation and, because we each have need of this, it is in the interest of each of us to be morally good: moral goodness is a kind of enlightened self-interest. But I do not wish to explore any of these thoughts. There is another version of the idea that the morally disreputable person is missing out on something crucial – crucially good – in life that I want to explore here. On this line of thought, what he is missing is precisely that something that we can all be presumed to want: happiness.

A very common way of proceeding these days is to draw on the writings of Aristotle who claimed that the virtuous life was central to the happy life. More exactly, Aristotle claimed that the life of ἀρετή (aretē) was necessary for the life of εὐδαιμονία (eudaimoniā). These Greek terms are often translated as 'virtue' and 'happiness' respectively. The latter is also often translated as 'well-being' or 'flourishing'. Hence it might be argued that the morally good life is the truly happy or flourishing life such that someone who is not morally good cannot be (truly) happy or cannot (truly) flourish. This might be so even if, as Aristotle granted, we also need things other than morality to be happy, such as health, certain material goods and the like. As Rosalind Hursthouse, a leading philosopher in the neo-Aristotelian revival in moral philosophy, often known as 'virtue ethics', puts it: 'All the usual versions of virtue ethics agree that living a life in accordance with virtue is necessary for *eudaimonia*.'[4]

On this view, the virtues are constitutive elements of *eudaimonia* or contribute to it in some necessary way. For example, in Alasdair MacIntyre's view of these things,[5] the virtues enable their possessor to take part in what he calls 'practices', by which he means, roughly speaking, socially established cooperative human activities that require and foster particular forms of human excellence, such as farming, the inquiries of the sciences, or the work of a painter or musician. Engagement in such activities gives rise to particular satisfactions which, accordingly, can be had only by those who possess the virtues. On this understanding of things, the virtues benefit their possessor. Hursthouse lists the following as virtues at various points in her book *On Virtue Ethics*: justice, honesty, charity or benevolence, courage, practical wisdom, generosity, loyalty, temperance, kindness and integrity.[6] The list is deliberately open-ended, and she may consider other traits of character to be virtues. Other virtue theorists consider the same kinds of character traits to be virtues. They are what one might call from this point of view 'common-sense moralists', taking their list of virtues from those kinds of traits of character that contemporary people in the West by and large tend to value.

However, what is at issue is not simply that for a life to be one of *eudaimonia* it must manifest some virtues, for just about any life does that, including some manifestly unhappy lives. After all, virtually everyone has at least some modicum of some of the virtues on the list – that is, virtually everyone is, to a greater or lesser extent, honest or loyal or kind or whatever, at least to some people in some contexts. Rather, the claim must be that for a life really to possess *eudaimonia* it must be in some overall sense dedicated to virtue or embody virtue as the central thing in life, manifesting these virtues in some striking or especially clear way. Otherwise, the claim is uninteresting for it puts no substantive constraints on what counts as a virtuous life: any person who did not in general lie, steal, cheat, kill and the like, and who was minimally kind or generous, would count as living in accord with virtue. This is quite contrary to Aristotle's view and, indeed, to that of mainstream moral philosophy since the Greeks, that the possession of virtue is a rare and difficult achievement.

Aristotle's argument for his view is long and complicated; we need not concern ourselves with all of it. Crucial for our purposes is that the problems start early on – start, indeed, with the terms Aristotle is using. We might translate ἀρετή as 'virtue' but really it has a meaning close to 'excellence', as many philosophers have pointed out. Aristotle gives us a thoroughly memorable description of the excellent person, the so-called proud or 'great-souled' man: this is the person who is *eudaimōn*, who possesses *eudaimonia*:

He is the sort of man to confer benefits, but he is ashamed of receiving them; for the one is the mark of a superior, the other of an inferior. And he is apt to confer greater benefits in return; for thus the original benefactor besides being paid will incur a debt to him, and will be the gainer by the transaction. [Such men] seem also to remember any service they have done, but not those they have received (for he who receives a service is inferior to him who has done it, but the proud man wishes to be superior), and to hear of the former with pleasure, of the latter with displeasure . . . It is a mark of the proud man also to ask for nothing or scarcely anything, but to give help readily, and to be dignified towards people who enjoy high position and good fortune, but unassuming towards those of the middle class; for it is a difficult and lofty thing to be superior to the former, but easy to be so to the latter, and a lofty bearing over the former is no mark of ill-breeding, but among humble people it is as vulgar as a display of strength against the weak. Again, it is characteristic of the proud man not to aim at the things commonly held in honour, or the things in which others excel; to be sluggish and to hold back except where great honour or a great work is at stake, and to be a man of few deeds, but of great and notable ones. He must also be open in his hate and in his love . . . and must speak and act openly; for he is free of speech because he is contemptuous, and he is given to telling the truth, except when he speaks in irony to the vulgar. He must be unable to make his life revolve round another, unless it be a friend; for this is slavish, and for this reason all flatterers are servile and people lacking in self-respect are flatterers. Nor is he given to admiration; for nothing to him is great. Nor is he mindful of wrongs; for it is not the part of a proud man to have a long memory, especially for wrongs, but rather to overlook them. Nor is he a gossip; for he will speak neither about himself nor about another, since he cares not to be praised nor for others to be blamed; nor again is he given to praise; and for the same reason he is not an evil-speaker, even about his enemies, except from haughtiness . . . He is one who will possess beautiful and profitless things rather than profitable and useful ones; for this is more proper to a character that suffices to itself.

Further, a slow step is thought proper to the proud man, a deep voice, and a level utterance; for the man who takes few things seriously is not likely to be hurried, nor the man who thinks nothing great to be excited, while a shrill voice and a rapid gait are the results of hurry and excitement.[7]

It is clear from this description that Aristotle's great-souled man, the perfect exemplar of the kind of life that he takes to be *eudaimōn*, is someone who is, to use a term employed much later by Nietzsche, *wohlgeraten* ('well turned-out'). That is clearly what Aristotle has in mind: the great-souled man is a kind of fine exemplar of the species, a magnificent tiger of a man.

We need to ask, first: is this kind of life, the life of the great-souled man, the only kind of truly excellent life? Second: is this life virtuous? Third: is this life a happy life?[8]

Even if you agree with Aristotle that the great-souled man's life is excellent, it hardly seems true that other kinds of human life are not. There is a programme on BBC Radio 4 entitled *Great Lives*. Each week, a guest chooses a person whom he or she admires and discusses that person with the presenter Matthew Parris and an expert on the subject's life. Subjects have included Byron, Gramsci, Rommel, the nineteenth-century bare-knuckle boxer Tom Spring, the soul singer James Brown, Schubert, Hemingway, the comedian Dave Allen, Brunel, Henry Purcell, Borges, Dante, Le Corbusier, Ava Gardner, the football manager Bill Shankly and numerous others. Clearly, those who choose such subjects think of their lives as excellent in various ways. Or we might think of Van Gogh, or Dostoevsky, or Beethoven, all of whom seem to me to have led excellent human lives. But in all these cases the lives in question are very different from the type of excellence that Aristotle had in mind. They are not even variants on that life, but something totally different. There are, surely, many different kinds of excellent life.

Moreover, it would be difficult to see all the lives I have mentioned as being especially virtuous. Virtue was not necessary for their excellence or the distinctive way in which they flourished. Van Gogh, for example, displayed a certain human excellence in his obsessive, tireless striving to find the artistic form that was adequate to what he wanted to create, but he was far from being a virtuous person. Again, Beethoven's life is surely excellent by any standard, but he was, in fact, far from virtuous: stubborn, proud, dogmatic and the like. This is not to deny that Van Gogh, Beethoven and the other individuals mentioned above possessed some virtue. But they were not, in the usual way in which we might say this, 'virtuous' people or in some way especially dedicated to virtue. It would be more realistic to say that what made their lives excellent was that they were doing what D. H. Lawrence recommended: 'Find your deepest impulse and follow that.' You could, of course, deny that the individuals whose lives are explored in the BBC programme flourished, and perhaps one might have reasonable doubts about some of them in this regard. But to deny that any of them flourished, or to say most of them did not, is surely not credible. Moreover, even if you think that Aristotle's great-souled man is excellent, it is hard to see him as especially virtuous – or, at any rate, he seems to have his fair share of vices. Indeed, by contemporary Western standards of virtue, he is a monster of bloated egoism and vanity. An excellent life, it seems, need not be an especially virtuous life.

It might be said that talking here of the excellent life is to miss the point. Aristotle is concerned with a kind of life that is *eudaimōn*, which means that it is not simply excellent but also happy. And, it might be said, Van Gogh and Beethoven were not very happy. That is true. But is Aristotle's great-souled man happy? Why should we think so? Could he not be all that Aristotle says he is, and yet miserable? He might be *eudaimōn*, flourishing, let us say, but unhappy in the sense of not having many positive or agreeable emotional states. It surely is just a fact that there are some people like Aristotle's great-souled man who are not happy, even if we think of them as flourishing. There is, therefore, no guarantee that this man is happy even if his life is excellent or flourishing. It is, after all, one of the most striking things about human beings that they can be dissatisfied even in the best of circumstances.

In fact, Aristotle insists that the life of virtue or excellence is pleasurable,[9] which we can take to mean happy. But

Aristotle does not seem to have a good reason for this claim. Or rather, it seems, he is assuming that the excellent or flourishing or virtuous life is one which is perfectly so, not only in the sense that the virtue is perfect but in the sense that this is a life in which being virtuous is always what the person in question wants to do, enjoys doing, something that flows from and expresses an inner harmony. For if it were not perfect in this way, then the person in question might have to struggle to be virtuous and that would surely not be pleasurable; it would impact negatively on his happiness. For sure, Aristotle acknowledges that there are some people who might be able to do the virtuous thing without being completely virtuous, and thus lack internal harmony, since to do this thing will be a struggle. But, as I have already mentioned, it is without doubt true that there is no such thing as a perfect person in the way Aristotle has in mind and never could be. His account at this point is totally unrealistic about what human beings are: the best of people, even the morally very best of people, are full of weaknesses, failings and the like, are very far from perfection. You could say that Aristotle is setting up an ideal and suggesting that we aim for it. This may be true and, in a way, is fair enough. But if you set up an ideal in this way, you must make it clear that you know that in the real world as it actually is no one will achieve that ideal. And that will mean, in the present context, that you will have to admit that no one can, in fact, achieve the kind of happiness in question. It is not just that virtue and thus *eudaimonia* are rare, as Aristotle granted. It seems that, on his account, they are impossible, though, no doubt, some might get significantly closer to them than others.

I have, then, suggested that an excellent or flourishing life need not be especially virtuous. But suppose we did, after all, for whatever reason, believe that only the virtuous life was an excellent life. Then we would be faced with this problem: which virtues? The kinds of virtues typical of, say, a Homeric warrior are not those of a medieval Christian monk or those of a modern bourgeois business manager. The warrior needs the kinds of virtues that are manifest in magnificent achievement and competition. The bourgeois citizen needs those virtues that allow for successful cooperation. Nor, for that matter, are the virtues required, say, of a modern professional sportsman or woman quite the same as those needed by a teacher or accountant or metalworker or fireman and so on. No doubt at some general level they all need, say, patience in one form or another, but the kind of patience required of a teacher is very different from that required by a fireman. There is no such thing as *the* virtuous life.

It is no doubt for this reason that, as Raymond Geuss has pointed out, from ancient philosophy onwards, the virtuous person was usually thought of as the person 'who has the cooperative bourgeois virtues of justice, truthfulness, self-restraint, and prudence'.[10] And we can certainly see something of this in the virtues that Hursthouse favours. After all, the following might also be thought of as virtues, in various different contexts, but Hursthouse does not speak of them as such: humility, asceticism, self-effacement, subservience, obedience, self-mortification; cunning, valour, virile dominance, personal honour, self-assertion, prowess. The problem is that the preference for a particular conception of bourgeois virtue is just that, a preference, not an understanding of virtue as such. If you say that the virtuous life is the flourishing life but then stipulate only a limited range of virtues as being relevant in this context, then you are clearly not arguing that the virtuous life is the flourishing life, but that a specific kind of virtuous life is such. But that will mean not simply that you are ruling out of court some examples of those who otherwise look as if they flourished, such as the monk or the Homeric warrior, but that you are showing a marked preference for a particular social order, that is, the one that sustains the kind of life you think of as flourishing. There is nothing wrong with having such a preference, of course, but the argument, in turning from being one in ethics to one in politics, will need to provide a justification for a particular political system.

I stated that *eudaimonia* is sometimes translated as 'happiness', and sometimes as 'flourishing' or 'well-being'. I suggested that a person could be *eudaimōn* without being happy. But if we understand *eudaimonia* as happiness, we run into problems immediately. No doubt each of us has some vague conception of what counts as happiness, but we are very far indeed from having anything like an agreed conception of what human happiness is. What might constitute happiness for you might be nothing like that which constitutes happiness for me. That is just an obvious fact about life, and the most we can say is that being happy *excludes* certain conditions such as misery, depression and the like, without our being able to say what, as such, it consists in.[11] Aristotle's great-souled man might be *eudaimōn* in the sense of flourishing and yet not happy. But if we say that he is happy after all, then the fact remains that being as he is might not make someone else happy. There are many different ways of being happy.

Moreover, one might come to think that the whole notion of whether one is happy or not is quite misleading. This is suggested by the opening passage of Hermann Hesse's novel *Gertrud*:

When I look back across my life from the outside, it does not seem especially happy. Nonetheless, I can with even less justice call it unhappy, despite all the errors. It is in the end also quite foolish to ask about happiness and unhappiness, for it seems to me that I would give up the unhappiest days of my life with more difficulty than all the cheerful ones. If in a human life the task is to accept the inevitable clearsightedly, to suffer good and evil fully, and to conquer an inner, more authentic, non-contingent destiny next to one's external destiny, then

> my life has been neither poor nor bad. If my external destiny has passed over me as over all other people, inevitably and as decreed by the gods, nonetheless my inner destiny has been my own work, whose sweetness or bitterness is mine, and for which I consider that I alone should accept the responsibility.[12]

In my view, there is something absolutely right in this: there is clearly something thoroughly adult in what Hesse is proposing here, in the sense that we could imagine a properly grown-up person believing it in all seriousness. Not everyone will look at life in this way, but there would be something foolish in refusing to take this view seriously. Yet many, such as Philippa Foot, who is, along with Hursthouse, a leading philosopher in modern neo-Aristotelian ethics, talk as if it were obvious that what human beings want in life is happiness.[13] It is not.

Be that as it may, in truth, we need to distinguish happiness from contentment, peace of mind, well-being, flourishing and no doubt much else besides, for these are all things that, at a general level, human beings might reasonably be supposed to want as central to a good life. A person might not be very happy in the sense of having many agreeable or pleasurable emotional states, but he might be quite content or possess peace of mind. Again, Dostoevsky or Wittgenstein, I am sure we should say, flourished as human beings, but they certainly were not very happy or content and notably lacked peace of mind. F. R. Leavis said this of Wittgenstein:

> Wittgenstein . . . was a complete human being, subtle, self-critical and un-self-exalting. When, in characterizing him, one touches on traits that seem to entail adverse or limiting judgements, one is not intending to impute defects in his potential full humanity.[14]

Then again, a happy life might not show much that we could understand as 'flourishing'; someone might lead a quiet, un-adventurous, timid, mediocre kind of life and be happy doing so, but hardly be flourishing in any significant way.

Should we say that the virtuous life – assuming we know what that is – is central to a life of happiness or to a life of contentment or to peace of mind? Which we say will depend upon, and make an enormous difference to, our understand-ing of the concept of virtue. Certain virtues might perhaps be (in part) constitutive of, or help lead towards, contentment, for example, but not at all to happiness.

In any case, some virtues can be bad for you or be a dis-advantage to possess and will undermine your happiness or contentment or possibility of flourishing. Sensitivity, kindness, gentleness, thoughtfulness, integrity and related virtues can well be harmful for their possessor, given the way the world is. If you reply that this is only true of excessive sensitivity and the like, thus of what are not truly the virtues, then that just seems to be wishful thinking: to suppose that the sensitivity that is bad for you is not true sensitivity is an idealization that does not look at what is there in the world. In truth, the gentle and kind are readily exposed to exploitation by others. The integrity of those who resist institutional corruption, complacency and apathy – these days often known as 'whistle-blowers' – is rarely rewarded and often punished. And those who are sensitive can be easily assailed by a sense of the world's harsh presence, as W. H. Auden remarked, speaking of the poet, but clearly with himself in mind:

> In our urbanized industrial society nearly everything we see and hear is so aggressively ugly or emphatically banal that it is difficult for a modern artist, unless he can flee to the depths of the country and never open a newspaper, to prevent his imagination from acquiring a Manichaean cast, from feeling, whatever his religious

convictions to the contrary, that the physical world is utterly profane or the abode of demons. However sternly he reminds himself that the material universe is the creation of God and found good by Him, his mind is haunted by images of physical disgust, cigarette butts in a half-finished sardine can, a toilet that won't flush etc.[15]

Simone de Beauvoir comments that Simone Weil, on hearing of the news of a famine in China, could not help but weep. 'I envied her for having a heart that could beat right across the world,' she wrote.[16] The less sensitive take all this in their stride. Yet Auden's sensitivity was most certainly a virtue and central to his artistic achievement, and Weil's compassion was key to her immense philosophical and spiritual achievements. Hursthouse writes that it is a 'fact that virtue is not unhealthy'.[17] The examples I have given suggest that in the case of some virtues, and from a psychological point of view, this is not so. Certainly the virtues can be painful to have and the world often delights in punishing you for having them.

Of course so-called virtue theorists, those who defend a neo-Aristotelian view of the virtues, can well grant that possessing the virtues can lead to loss, as when courage in battle leads the soldier to his or her death. It is certainly true that, owing to force of circumstance, the virtues can lead their possessor into disaster. If the virtues benefit their possessor they do so generally, not on every single occasion. Hence Hursthouse writes that 'possession of the virtues [does not guarantee] . . . that one will flourish. The claim is that they are the only reliable bet – even though, it is agreed, I might be unlucky and, precisely because of my virtue, wind up dying early or with my life marred or ruined.'[18] I accept the point, indeed am myself claiming that the virtues can lead one into disaster, though I think that the theorists badly underestimate how frequently this is likely to occur. Be that as it may, that is only part of the point I wish to make. I am also saying that the virtues can themselves be harmful to possess in that they *expose* one horribly in and to the world. The gentle and kind, those who are sensitive and possess integrity, are likely to find the world painful as such, even if, by good fortune, they escape the marauding attentions of others. Possessing the virtues can make the world a difficult place to be. It is striking in this context that Aristotle's great-souled man possesses the kinds of virtues that fit him to be well protected from the world in this sense, possesses, that is, a kind of toughness – he is *not* sensitive, kind, gentle or thoughtful. Or again, if you think that the virtues are those traits of character that facilitate successful bourgeois cooperation, you are likely not to see so clearly the ways in which possessing the virtues can be bad for their possessor. But, as I have already pointed out, there is no such thing as *the* virtuous life and Aristotle's conception of virtue or the bourgeois conception are only two of various possibilities and cannot claim to exhaust our sense of what a virtuous life might be.

Beyond all that, there is clearly something mistaken about supposing that it is only to a person's character that we should look to get a sense of the excellence of the life. Hannah Arendt expresses this point by saying that we need to distinguish *who* one is from *what* one is, where the latter concerns a description one might give of a person, and, however detailed and accurate that description might be, the person's reality, *who* he is, will escape it. The *who* is the indefinable identity of a person, experienced primarily in the particularity of his presence to us, but also there in what we sense as the spirit in which he lives or lived. Arendt expresses the point in this way:

> The manifestation of who the speaker and doer un-
> exchangeably is, though it is plainly visible, retains a
> curious intangibility that confounds all effort towards
> unequivocal verbal expression. The moment we want

> to say *who* somebody is our very vocabulary leads us astray into saying *what* he is; we get entangled in a description of qualities he necessarily shares with others like him; we begin to describe a type or 'character' . . . with the result that his specific uniqueness escapes us.[19]

Dostoevsky, for example, was in some ways a foolish person, miserably in love with his younger wife, the victim of a gambling obsession, morbid in his desire to control his wife's behaviour and so on. We could say that he flourished in his professional but not his personal life. But it is better and more realistic to say that he did indeed flourish as a human being but that this was less a matter of his character – though that is relevant, of course – than one of the whole manner or spirit in which he led his life, *who* he was. Leavis is saying the same thing about Wittgenstein, which is why, for Leavis, his defects do not undermine his 'full humanity'. A more literal translation of Aristotle's term εὐδαιμονία is something like 'good spirit'. So we might say that the excellent life is a life lived in a good spirit. Dostoevsky and Wittgenstein lived excellent lives in a good spirit. This is, in my view, clearly true, despite their many forms of foolishness and failure – or perhaps even in part because of their foolishness and failure, which no doubt contributed in various ways to their depth as individuals because they helped to give them a sense of human existence in all its complexity and recalcitrance. It is also true despite the fact that they were far from being especially virtuous.

In the light of the points I have made, it seems to me quite clear that there is very little hope at all of showing that living a life in accordance with virtue is necessary for happiness (or flourishing), as Aristotle believed, even if one also accepts, as did Aristotle, that certain external goods are also necessary for such a life – health and certain material possessions, for example. Still less is there hope of showing, as Plato hoped to, that virtue was necessary and sufficient for the good life, that is, that virtue is the only thing that matters. It is, surely, a terrible moralization of human life to suppose that a person who is abused and tortured remains happy or flourishing if he keeps his virtue. And Aristotle's view is, in the end, not much better. He considers whether, for example, King Priam of Troy, whose city is destroyed by the Greeks and whose son, Hector, is slain by Achilles – Achilles then desecrates the body – loses his *eudaimonia*. Priam pleads with Achilles to return the body, saying: 'I have endured what no one on earth has ever done before – I put my lips to the hands of the man who killed my son.' Aristotle draws a distinction between a happy and a blessed life: the former is one that is virtuous while the latter is such a life that is also marked by good fortune, certainly untouched by the kind of personal disaster to which Priam was subject. Aristotle's verdict on Priam is thus that 'the happy man can never become miserable; though it is true he will not be supremely blessed if he encounters the misfortunes of a Priam', though he also seems to have doubts about this conclusion, saying: 'No one calls a man happy who meets with misfortunes like Priam's.'[20] The latter verdict is more plausible. But one might have hoped that Aristotle would say more directly and cleanly what seems obviously true, namely, that such a man's life is ruined. And this is so even if he bears his sufferings nobly. Indeed, if he does bear his sufferings nobly, that may make it all the more apparent that his life has been ruined. The fact that Aristotle does not make the point more directly shows how much he wishes to preserve his thesis. And, in any case, given that Priam's sufferings were almost unimaginably bad, it is clear that Aristotle would think that most sufferings could not affect one's *eudaimonia*, assuming that one is virtuous. No doubt many who defend an Aristotelian view would be less sanguine than he is in this regard, according more weight to the necessity of external goods for *eudaimonia*, but surely the point is that the way of proceeding in question gets things the wrong way round. If we start from wishing to argue that virtue makes for *eudaimonia*, we then have to think about which negative events in life might threaten that connection so construed. It is more realistic, surely, to start from the idea that human beings need lots of things for *eudaimonia*, among which virtue is just one element; important, no doubt, but small nonetheless.

For the most we can say, I think, is that all human beings have need of some modicum of virtue, whatever they do, 'as bees need their stings', but that the possession of such virtue is, at best, one small part of the many and various things that human beings need to achieve whatever, as individuals, they might prefer by way of contentment, flourishing, well-being or happiness. After all, even thieves and the corrupt and those who exploit also need their share of the so-called cardinal virtues, that is, courage, temperance, prudence and justice. A totally cowardly thief, for example, would be a hopeless thief, as Genet, who spent the first part of his life as a thief and who knew many thieves personally, explored at length. But that, of course, does nothing at all to show that virtue is necessary for happiness or flourishing, because the life of a thief is not a virtuous life – which was part of its immense attraction for Genet. And, more generally, human beings need character traits that are not virtues at all, such as, depending on their situation, ebullience, humour, imagination, clear-headedness, eloquence, efficiency, charisma, perseverance, elegance, resourcefulness, eagerness, playfulness, urbanity, warmth, tractability, depth, thoroughness, vivacity, glamour, attentiveness, insouciance, independence, curiosity, resilience, poise, level-headedness, tact, passion, eccentricity . . . You could, of course, insist that these are all virtues, but that would empty the concept of any substantive content, leaving any character trait of which you approved, or which helped individuals be successful in life, as a virtue. And, further, human beings need much else besides: food, water, shelter, pleasure, play and relaxation of various kinds, health in whatever way they think of it, generally favourable material circumstances, support from others in various ways, favourable political conditions free from oppression and a great deal of luck. Virtue is, at best, a small part of the good life.

Certainly the whole argument concerning virtue and happiness (or flourishing) can be salvaged by acknowledging that the conception of happiness in question is value-laden, that is, expresses a conception of what is truly or really worth having. On this line of thought, someone who does not possess the virtues, who does not live in such a way as to show that his life is dedicated to virtue, almost certainly will not see the point of having them and will not appreciate that the kind of happiness in question is true or real happiness. In that sense, we could just *define* Aristotle's great-souled man – or some other person manifesting your favourite version of the life of virtue, such as those virtues that suit one for bourgeois cooperation – as leading a *eudaimōn* life. In one way, this is a reasonable strategy: the person who is thoroughly wicked and does not care a fig for moral considerations cannot be expected to be convinced by any argument seeking to show the importance of morality in life. In this sense it is true that, as philosophers often put it, morality does not admit of external justification. But in another way, as directed against someone who does care for moral considerations but who thinks, as I have been urging, that it is implausible to suppose that a virtuous life is especially significant for *eudaimonia*, the idea that there is no external justification for morality looks suspiciously like an attempt to secure a conclusion by insulating philosophical reflection from contact with a world that would undermine it.

Those who disagree with my line of reflection would say that their view of the virtues is grounded in a conception of human nature. It might be said, for example, that human beings are by nature social animals and that the virtues are, at least in part, those dispositions of character that enable them to live in social groups. Since living in social groups is good for them because it fulfils their nature, we can argue, so the thought goes, that possessing the relevant virtues is good for them and contributes to their happiness.

However, there are, I think, two major problems with this argument. The first is that human beings can live in a vast variety of different social groups and many of these – many in which they have actually lived – do little to contribute to the well-being of many or most of their inhabitants. In deeply hierarchical and inegalitarian societies, the kind of character traits needed by most are those that enable them to obey will-ingly or passively, to accept their lot and stay put. It is unlikely that this will be thought to be the kind of thing that those defending the role of the virtues in the happy life will want to accept. But if they say that a more egalitarian kind of society allows all its members to flourish, then this will be true on a conception of flourishing that is clearly not grounded in the fact that human beings are social animals – which was supposed to be the point of appealing to our social nature. It will be grounded, rather, in their *preferred* conception of the social. The argument will have become question-begging.

The second problem is this. Even if it is true that human beings are social animals, they are not all social in the same way. Perhaps no human being can live wholly outside of contact with others – and this is certainly true of infants and children – but it is clearly true that some individuals need the virtues that enable them to live in social groups to a much lesser extent than others. Loners, recluses, highly independent people and so on simply do not need the same social virtues as do highly gregarious individuals. It follows that we cannot argue from the fact that human beings are social animals to claim that they all need a certain set of virtues because having these virtues contributes to their flourishing. The most we can claim is that enough human beings in any given group need just enough of those kinds of virtues that keep the group going. That is nowhere near the strong claim that that the argument was supposed to show plausible.

There might, of course, be other ways of seeking to show that the virtuous life is grounded in, is the best or proper development of, our nature. But it seems to me that such a view will always fail because it will, indeed, be value-laden or evaluatively loaded. Of course there are different views on what our nature is, assuming we have one. I think we do have a nature but that, if we look without prejudice at human beings, we shall see that any account of what we are will have to accept that we are, by nature, unstable, violent, aggressive, greedy creatures, creatures whose mind is, as Bernard Williams put it, in many deep ways an inhospitable location for goodness.[21] We may also be, as Hume pointed out, by nature given to certain reactions of sympathy or empathy, but any view that seeks, as the virtue theory view does, to give an account of what it is to flourish in a distinctively or characteristically human way is likely to end up having to acknowledge that to flourish in a characteristically human way is to be violent, aggressive or greedy in those ways that are distinctive of human beings. For sure, we might also say that to flourish in this way is also to manifest the distinctive human capacity for empathy, but only by having a wildly optimistic view of human nature could one suppose that it is in the life of virtue that human beings flourish in a characteristically human way.

The truth seems to me to be this: on the one hand, we value morality and, on the other, we value happiness, contentment, flourishing and so on. But they overlap only partially and in complicated ways. The good life for a human being involves some, at least minimal, commitment to some virtues, but the answer to the question 'Why be moral?' is not to be found in the claim that only in this way can one be happy or flourish as a human being.

It might seem that there are some philosophers whose work in ethics is deeply indebted to Aristotle who would nonetheless agree with my conclusion. Philippa Foot, for example, grants that the wicked can flourish like the bay tree, and, in granting this, she takes issue with John McDowell, who also draws heavily on Aristotle, and who, as Foot says, seems to identify the life of virtue with happiness.[22] Moreover, Hursthouse, consistently with her view that possessing the virtues is the 'best bet' for a flourishing life, also grants that the wicked can flourish but says that this no more undermines the claim that virtue is the best bet for achieving a flourishing life than does the fact that there are a few people who drink and smoke heavily until a ripe old age undermine my doctor's advice to me to drink in moderation and give up smoking. To follow his advice is still the best bet for a flourishing life.[23]

There are, however, two issues here. One is whether the wicked can flourish. The other is whether the virtues are the best bet for achieving a life of *eudaimonia* – flourishing, happiness and so on. It is true that the wicked can flourish. But the real issue is not that but what to say about all the ordinary people who are not wicked at all, but are morally average, leading normally decent, morally acceptable lives, in which they manifest some virtues and also the normal human failings, weaknesses, forms of veniality and the like – the normal ruck of human beings, you and me, for example, and the people by whom we are surrounded, such as colleagues, family and friends. Such people are not committed to the virtuous life in any particularly striking way, though they do take moral concerns, among other things, seriously. Are they living a life in accordance with virtue? If we say yes, then the constraints on what counts as living such a life are very weak. On such a reading, the claim that virtue is necessary for *eudaimonia* would be tantamount to the claim that not being a morally nasty person – the kind of person who is just mean, selfish and thoughtless – is a necessary condition for *eudaimonia* or the 'best bet' for *eudaimonia*. But, whatever else we think about that idea, it is hardly the strong and impressive claim with which the argument began. Moreover, it would result in the conclusion that pretty much most people, that is, ordinarily morally decent people, possess *eudaimonia*, which would turn out to be, after all, a fairly average kind of state. That would mean that most ordinary and ordinarily decent people would fulfil the requirements for *eudaimonia* – living in accordance with virtue – rather easily. The claim that virtue is necessary for *eudaimonia* would thus not be a controversial or especially interesting idea for which it might be worth arguing, but, rather, more or less a description of the way most ordinary, unexceptional but decent people are. It would also be consistent with my view that virtue is at best only a small part of what human beings need to achieve *eudaimonia*.

In other words, this notion that the life of virtue and thus the possession of *eudaimonia* are fairly easy to achieve simply cannot be what any modern virtue theorist can want to assert. In fact, the more plausible thing for such thinkers to say is, as Aristotle says, that virtue is rare or even, as I suggested earlier, impossible, and thus that most people do not flourish or are not happy or do not achieve well-being, depending on how one interprets *eudaimonia*. One could, of course, suggest, as I have, that some are closer to it than others.

Now this, given the view for which I have provided reasons earlier in this book that human beings are creatures who are deeply in conflict with themselves, is an independently plausible theory. That is, if what we mean by *eudaimonia* is 'happiness', then it seems to be true that most people are not, indeed, happy, although, of course, they do have moments or periods of happiness. Nonetheless, it seems to me clear that some human beings really do flourish or lead excellent lives, but that that is completely consistent with their lives being in some significant ways, including moral ways, a failure or a mess, not least since such failure or mess – as I mentioned in the case of Wittgenstein and Dostoevsky – can contribute to the depth or wisdom of such people. To put the point polemically or even paradoxically: if there were any such thing as a perfect person, even morally perfect, he or she would be full of moral failings. This is a point entirely missed by Aristotle and also by many of those who follow him. And the root problem seems to be that Aristotle and those who follow him do not seem to have an adequate understanding of the fact that *all* human beings are, in various ways, to various degrees, a *mess*. They seem to have no sense of Orwell's point, quoted earlier, that 'any life when viewed from the inside is simply a series of defeats,' or that, as Eliot has it, 'The best of a bad job is all any of us make of it.' If we are properly to understand human happiness or flourishing or well-being or contentment or peace of mind or the like then we have to start from *that* if what we are going to say is realistic. Virtue and its role in happiness will look quite different if we do. Those who, like Aristotle, do not start there end up with a quite unrealistic account of how virtue fits in with these things.

Some virtue theorists do accept that virtue is rare. But I am not sure whether they would be happy to accept the claim that human beings rarely possess *eudaimonia*. Surely they ought to reject it. For, if part of the aim of virtue theory is to show how it is that one can have a reason to be morally good because the virtuous life is the life of *eudaimonia*, and it turns out that it is extremely difficult to achieve virtue and thus that *eudaimonia* is largely elusive, then the whole argument collapses. No reason will have been given why one ought to be moral, except, perhaps, for those who are prepared to set themselves the task of a relentless pursuit of virtue as the most important thing in life. For the rest of us the argument will look like a species of moralizing in the negative sense of the term and be discouraging, raising, perhaps, the suspicion that morality is, after all, for the frail creatures such as we are, a kind of fraud or con. It is significant in this context that, in a study of

Aristotle's ethics, Jonathan Lear does, indeed, arrive at the conclusion that Aristotle's ethics implies that virtually no one achieves *eudaimonia*.[24] Evidently, that was not the conclusion that Aristotle wanted or thought he had arrived at. And it will not help to be told that the rest of us, even if we do not possess complete virtue or *eudaimonia*, possess these in part. For the point is that the argument is still telling us that a central reason for our possessing these only partially is that we do not accord enough value to virtue, stubbornly going on seeing other things as just as, or more, important than virtue.

Hursthouse would certainly reply to my argument that the virtues form at best only a small part of what any human being needs to flourish or be happy by saying that the fact that we bring our children up to be as virtuous as possible shows that we think that the virtues benefit their possessor. In doing this, we might say, we are seeking to benefit our children and make as sure as we can that life goes well for them.

I have already granted that we all need some measure of virtue. To that extent I agree with Hursthouse. However, although we do, indeed, seek to inculcate in our children the virtues, we can be glad that our efforts at least partly fail in this regard. For it is obvious that, if we want our children to be kind, generous, sensitive, thoughtful and the like, we can also be glad that they turn out to be, *just as we are ourselves*, in various ways insensitive, indifferent, thoughtless and the like, for only in being such can they – can we – live in a world whose demands on us from a moral point of view would otherwise be unbearable. Only our indifference and insensitivity allows us to ignore the hundreds of millions of starving people in the world, the pain and suffering of victims of torture and other forms of abuse, the misery of poverty and poor opportunity faced by countless millions, the impending catastrophe of climate change and the like, about which we could be doing something right now, instead of writing or reading a book in philosophy, that is, doing something that ministers to our limited and egotistical aims, or, if you want to put this more generously, that helps us to make something of our own life. You can certainly insist that it is morally legitimate to get on with one's own life while ignoring the plight of others. No doubt this is true. But it is important to see that the kinds of traits of character that allow one to exercise that morally legitimate goal involve those which betoken our insensitivity and thoughtlessness. We simply do not think about the kinds of things I have mentioned most of the time, and that is what that insensitivity and that thoughtlessness allow us to do.

Foot, incidentally, is also interested, and rightly so since it is a very important issue, in the fact that there are some people who could not achieve happiness through wicked actions.[25] This is certainly true – Macbeth is one such example – but does nothing to show that, after all, the virtuous life is necessary for happiness. It shows something else: that some people could not live with themselves having done something wicked, that their happiness (or flourishing) is not to be found in wickedness. That is entirely consistent with the claims I have made in this chapter. We all have limits, things which, were we to do them, would prevent us from being able to live with ourselves afterwards in peace. And each person's limits are his or her own. A completely average person, whose life is not especially virtuous and is full of the usual compromises that characterize any human life, and who finds his happiness in much besides virtue, might be unable to do some wicked deed, such as betraying a friend. But that does nothing to support Hursthouse's claim that 'living a life in accordance with virtue is necessary for *eudaimonia*.' It just shows that he has reached a limit. No doubt there are some whose limits in this sense are, so to speak, extremely rigorous, in that they set for themselves the task of being morally upright all the time and never finding their happiness in anything but virtue. But that, too, does nothing to support Hursthouse's claim. There are two quite different things at issue here: the idea that we each have moral limits and the claim that virtue is necessary to happiness. You cannot claim that the former fact does anything to support the latter.

Among philosophers of the classical tradition, Kant would have agreed with my conclusion. He emphasized strongly, and in opposition to Greek philosophy, the disjunction between happiness and moral goodness, insisting that it was quite clear that in this world there is no correlation of reason or desert between our moral worth and what we enjoy or suffer. He did not think that the virtues benefit their possessor or that the best bet for a happy or flourishing life is to be virtuous. He thought that we are required to be morally good because that is a demand of reason, and that whether that leads to our being happy or not is neither here nor there. But Kant's view is in the minority among philosophers. It is not just – despite the point that Hursthouse and Foot make about the wicked flourishing – that in general, as Nietzsche put it, 'the wicked who are happy are a species about whom the moralists are silent.'[26] It is also that philosophers have, generally speaking, not paid much attention to – certainly have not, in the main, explored in detail – the fact that virtue has only a small part to play in human happiness and that virtue, moral goodness, really only has a little to do with whether any given person is happy or miserable, leads a good life or suffers a lot. Or, if they have paid attention to this, it has usually been, as in the Aristotelian tradition, to try to show that it is not true that virtue is relatively insignificant for human happiness.

Why is this? At a general level, no doubt, one thing that is relevant is that virtually all of us like to suppose that morality matters more to us than it in fact does; such a supposition flatters us. Virtue ethics encourages such a view and is thus likely to be appealing to the image it pleases us to have of ourselves. Be that as it may, it seems to me that crucial here is the idea that there is something unbearable for the human mind in the thought that morality and happiness come apart in the way I have suggested they do. Indeed, I want to suggest that this is a kind of tragic knowledge. But while we may know this, we find it almost impossible to acknowledge it. There is something in us that *demands* that virtue and happiness go together and it is a kind of affront to our sense of the world that this is not so. Children naturally assume this to be the case, and it is part of the painful transition to adulthood that we accept that this is not the case. Simone de Beauvoir expresses this assumption clearly in her reflections on her childhood:

> The two major categories according to which my universe organised itself were Good and Evil. I occupied the region of the Good where, indissolubly united, reigned happiness and virtue. I had already the experience of unjustified pain: I had knocked and grazed myself; I had had an attack of ecthyma, and a doctor had had to cauterise the pustules with silver nitrate, which made me cry. But these accidents were soon put right and did not shake my credo: the joys and tears of human beings correspond to their moral worth.[27]

We all live with a sense of how the world *ought* to be, in various ways, and key to that is the thought that it ought to be such that virtue and happiness go together and that the response to the evil is not a mere indifferent universe which means that the wicked can flourish. We all share Beauvoir's thought that 'the joys and tears of human beings correspond to their moral worth', or ought to. Think how readily the thought that they are being punished for something comes to those who are diagnosed with cancer and you will see the point. It is on account of such thoughts as these that Samuel Johnson, for example, found the death of Cordelia unbearable because here is a person who embodies goodness and yet she is ground up in the indifferent workings of the world and the malign workings of her sisters. The so-called 'happy ending' is not simply a Hollywood cliché: it is an expression of a deep need we have to see justice done; our feelings and sentiment call out for a resolution that fits with our moral aspirations.

Nonetheless, it seems to me that we are also dealing here, in part at least, with the tense relations between philosophy and tragedy of which I spoke earlier in this book. Philosophy wants things to make sense, and tragedy says that they do not. What we know of human history is that it is a scene of the most relentless barbarity, cruelty, savagery and utterly pointless suffering, and part of that is most certainly the destruction of those good people who deserved much better and the triumph of the brutal who deserved less than they got. Part of philosophy's insistence on connecting virtue and happiness as it so often does is to help us avert our eyes from the horror of human history – from the tragedy of human experience. We are dealing here with what Bernard Williams called 'the defective consciousness of moral philosophy', which 'is deeply attached to giving good news' and which has the 'tireless aim of . . . [seeking] to make the world safe for well-disposed people'. He thought this might be helped by reflection on such a play as Sophocles' *The Women of Trachis*: 'All the force of the play is directed to leaving in the starkest relief its extreme, undeserved and uncompensated suffering.'[28] Perhaps.

* * *

Part of what we are longing for when we long for virtue and happiness to go together is for the world to be, in the end, in some way, even if we cannot fully understand it, as it *ought* to be. We are longing for a moral world order. Of course, when we act morally we act in some local way, seeking to improve the world in some very specific respect. But, implicitly or explicitly, what we want is not simply that we succeed here, at the local level, but that our efforts somehow have an impact in making the world as such what we think it ought to be, for that is another expression of our longing for a moral world order. For those who believe in the Christian God that hope can be justified because history is, in the Christian perspective, teleological and is working towards a redemptive goal in which there will be a final triumph of a moral world order through God's agency. This is, indeed, why hope is one of the theological virtues: through it the Christian can trust that his local moral efforts contribute to making the world as it ought to be. But for those who do not have such belief, the longing does not go away. It is just that it cannot be answered by any idea about the Christian God.

What we put in his place is the idea of modernity as a site or place of increasing and inevitable moral progress, a kind of progress that redeems history. The theological virtue of hope is replaced by the secular optimism of a belief in progress. We are helped to see part of what is at stake here by one of the great reflections on modern moral consciousness, Kleist's novella *Michael Kohlhaas*, based on the true story of one man's longing for justice.[29]

Kohlhaas, who is described as a man with a sense of justice 'as fine as a gold balance', is a horse dealer in Brandenburg and one day, while leading a team of horses to market in Saxony, he is stopped by an official of Junker Wenzel von Tronka who tells him he does not have the necessary legal documents to continue. This is news to Kohlhaas, who has passed this way many times, and he manages to persuade the official to let him continue on condition that he leave two of his horses on the Junker's estate, along with one of his young employees who is charged with looking after the horses. Kohlhaas later discovers that the official's claim that he needed such papers was wholly false, and he is enraged when he discovers that his employee has been beaten and his horses exhausted by being put to work in the Junker's fields. This sets in train Kohlhaas's attempt to obtain justice and, finding himself frustrated at every turn, as well as having to endure the death of his wife, who is killed accidentally while seeking to plead her husband's case, he ends up embarking on a campaign of pillaging and looting, all in the name of justice, which ends in his own execution at the moment in which the horses are finally returned to him.

One of the things that Kleist wants to show in his novella is that there is a sense in which what Kohlhaas wants is for his achieving justice not simply to bring about this local good but to help change the world in a fundamental way by making it just. That is, even if his desire for justice is satisfied, this is not enough for him, for that changes nothing beyond the local level: the world continues to be unjust, and corruption continues to be rife, even though the one case has been settled in his favour.

Kleist tells us this in pointing out that, at one point, Kohlhaas seeks to proclaim a new world order. Working here is Kleist's sense of what the world order – or rather, world disorder – already is. He speaks in this context of what he called '*die gebrechliche Einrichtung der Welt*', the faulty or imperfect structure or set-up of the world. The word he uses in this context, *Einrichtung*, is revealing, since it can also be used in German when one speaks of, for example, the set-up or arrangement of a room – its furniture, for example. But at the same time as it carries this intimate, domestic connotation, it also has the metaphysical resonance exploited by Kleist, that is, as pointing towards something fundamental in human beings' condition. Kleist is inviting us into a view of our condition as follows. The world is not as we want it to be, for it is, among other things, unjust. We seek to make local improvements to the world, to ameliorate the human condition, but these local improvements can never change the basic features of the world, which remains unjust and is never as we think it *ought* to be. So, Kleist is saying, while our local improvements are something that we want, they are also something that will necessarily disappoint us: they can never fulfil the promise they hold out that they will allow us to make over the world into what we think it ought to be. In this sense, there is no room for hope in the world as Kleist portrays it.

Nietzsche addressed the same issue in his discussion of Hamlet in *The Birth of Tragedy*, providing an interpretation of Hamlet's well-known incapacity to act, his inability to avenge his father's death, in such terms. Comparing Hamlet to what he calls the 'Dionysian man', that is, the person who has seen through to the nature of reality, Nietzsche writes:

> The Dionysian man bears a similarity to Hamlet: both have had a real glimpse into the essence of things. They have *understood*, and it disgusts them to act, for their action can change nothing in the eternal nature of things. They find it ridiculous or humiliating that they might be expected to order again a world which is out of joint. Knowledge kills action, for action requires our being covered with the veil of illusion – that is what Hamlet has to teach . . . Now any consolation no longer has an effect. His longing goes out over a world, even beyond the gods themselves, towards death. Existence, along with its blazing reflection in the gods or in an immortal afterlife, is denied. In the consciousness of once having glimpsed the truth, man now sees every-where only the horror or absurdity of being; now he understands the symbolism in the fate of Ophelia; now he recognizes the wisdom of the forest god Silenus. It disgusts him.[30]

But Nietzsche was himself like this. Noting that we want the world, as such, to be other than it is, that we think it *ought* to be other than it is, but that we are deprived of the theological hope that it really will be, he believed that this desire expressed a kind of denial of things as they are – 'life denial', he called it. And in a way he is right, of course, because without hope in the theological sense we cannot believe that the world can ever really be fundamentally other than it is, and so to reject it as it is is to reject all that it is and could be. In the Christian scheme, on the other hand, to reject the world as it is now is simply to reject its present manifestation, for it will change.

Tormented by this life denial and determined to avoid it, he sought to affirm life as it actually was, that is, to excise the 'moral ought' from the world or, to put it another way, to live entirely without hope. So in his writings he again and again sought ways of simply accepting suffering, his own and others': to accept all suffering, he thought, was to refuse to moralize it, to refuse to think that there was anything wrong when, for example, the good suffered and the evil flourished. In fact, to excise the moral ought would be to excise that thought put in that way, since, if there were no moral ought, no way the world ought to be, then one could not even think that the good ought to be happy and the evil miserable. There would simply be the fact of people existing, some happy and some unhappy, but no way they ought – *morally* ought – to be. Hence he celebrated those who, he supposed (no doubt with a fair dose of artistic licence), could look at things this way – Napoleon, Cesare Borgia and others – and celebrated ages which accepted human suffering much more readily than modernity. And he longed to be like this himself, which is why there are passages in Nietzsche's work in which he shows himself to be fascinated by violence. Whatever else is the case, he is here seeking to make himself hard, as he supposed Napoleon and the rest to be, because he believed that unless one were that one could not bear life and would have to deny it – which would be a denial of everything. Nietzsche was himself a rather gentle, somewhat timid man, with an acutely sensitive moral consciousness that led him to feel sharply the pain of the world, and it is precisely *because* of this that his work so often seems to celebrate violence; the contradiction is only apparent because the former explains the latter. His gentleness would naturally have led him (in his terms) to deny life, and that was why he sought to rid himself of it.

Nietzsche is haunted by the idea that, unless some local improvement – however this might be understood – helps to change everything, to give a new conception of life such as to change it in its fundamental nature, one can only be led into resignation or despair. That is a way of saying, of course, that he had no hope, that he had lost all hope in the sense of a theological virtue. He is, of course, like many of us in that way.

For Nietzsche, therefore, there are two options: either we excise the moral ought from the world altogether, reject morality and accept the world as it is; or we become what he calls moral fanatics, seeking to subsume all value to moral value and turn the world into a morally perfect place. Either of these possibilities, if realized, would make the world into what we think it ought to be, because in either case we would precisely no longer have the thought that the world ought to be other than it is. Neither can be realized, but a simulacrum of the latter is possible in the idea of modernity as a place of inevitable moral progress, as on the way to being morally perfect. Or, to the put the point as I did earlier, the idea of moral progress together with its attendant optimism replaces God and the theological virtue of hope.

What Kleist, in the figure of Kohlhaas, and Nietzsche help us see is our fractured relation to morality in the modern world. Without a conception of modernity as a scene or site of secure moral progress, we are likely to believe that our local efforts at moral engagement do nothing to contribute to making the world as we think it ought to be. But if the world is such a scene, then we can believe that our local efforts do, after all, contribute to changing the world as such – the eternal nature of things, as Nietzsche puts it – even if the change is not immediate. And that gives us a substitute for hope in the theological sense and helps us avoid a sense of anguish or despondency. The character Stepan, in Camus' *Les Justes*, expresses it thus: 'For us, who do not believe in God, justice must be total or there is only despair.'[31] It is as if Nietzsche replied to this: 'Yes, but total justice is impossible, so to avoid despair we have to get rid altogether of the very idea of justice.' But modernity sides with Stepan, not Nietzsche. Henry Staten makes the point about modernity's investment in the idea of a perfect justice in this way:

> What are we to say about this [history's] overwhelming spectacle of cruelty, stupidity, and suffering? What stance is there for us to adopt with respect to history, what judgment can we pass on it? Is it all a big mistake? Christianity attempted to recuperate the suffering of history by projecting a divine plan that assigns it a reason in the here and now and a recompense later, but liberalism is too humane to endorse this explanation. There is no explanation, only the brute fact. But the brute fact we are left with is even harder to stomach than the old explanation. So Left liberalism packages it in a new narrative, a moral narrative according to which all those lives ground up in the machinery of history are assigned an intelligible role as victims of oppression and injustice . . . Against the awesome 'Thus it was' of history we set the overawing majesty of 'Thus it ought to have been'.[32]

It ought to have been as it is now – or will be soon when the final prejudices have been excised from the world. That thought is central to modern moral consciousness. If I am right, it works to save us from despair at the thought that our local moral efforts change nothing in the world: it gives us an optimism that replaces the hope that God will bring good out of evil and that we shall finally live in a world that is as it ought to be.

* * *

There are other lessons to be drawn from Kleist. One concerns the relation between virtue and vice, for Kleist makes it clear that Kohlhaas becomes a murderer and bandit only because he has such a fine sense of justice. What Kleist helps us see is that we live with a myth. The myth is that the virtues are wholly opposed to the vices. But this is not true: the virtues are nourished by the vices. As La Rochefoucauld puts it in his *Maxims*: 'The vices enter into the composition of the virtues as poison enters into the composition of medicines. Prudence assembles and tempers them, and uses them against the ills of life.'[33] Vanity and self-love enter into all kinds of virtues, helping to make them what they are. Of course, as La Rochefoucauld insists, they have to be tempered, or channelled and educated, but this is not the same thing as extirpating them. There is an egoistic force that underlies much virtue and moral goodness, the egoistic force that animates and nourishes love, friendship, creative activity in various forms – artistic, scientific, sporting and so on – attachment to this or that noble or decent project, the desire to please and the like. Indeed, without this egoistic energy, those things we value so much, such as love, would not be possible. As Auden said: 'Every artist knows that the sources of his art are what Yeats called "the foul rag-and-bone-shop of the heart", its lusts, its hatreds, its envies.'[34] What is true of the artist's art is true also of the rest of the things we value in life. George Orwell makes the point in his essay 'Why I Write'. He gives his first reason:

> *Sheer egoism.* Desire to seem clever, to be talked about, to be remembered after death, to get your own back on the grown-ups who snubbed you in childhood, etc., etc. It is humbug to pretend this is not a motive, and a strong one. Writers share this characteristic with scientists, artists, politicians, lawyers, soldiers, successful businessmen.[35]

Orwell seems to me to be wrong only in not making clear that the kind of egoism of which he speaks is to be found everywhere, not just among the kinds of persons he mentions, helping to motivate the things we value.

An excellent example is to be found in C. S. Lewis's wonderful little book *A Grief Observed*, in which he seeks to come to terms with his agony at the death of his wife, whom he calls in the book 'H'. What Lewis sees again and again in the book is the way in which his love for his wife was in many ways deeply egoistical. About a quarter of the way into his notes, for example, he writes:

> For the first time I have looked back and read these notes. They appal me. From the way I have been talking anyone would think that H's death mattered chiefly for its effect on myself. Her point of view seems to have dropped out of sight.[36]

Again he worries that 'the notes [he has been making] have been about myself, and about H., and about God. In that order. The order and proportions exactly what they ought not to have been'.[37] And:

> What sort of lover am I to think so much about my affliction and so much less about hers? Even the insane call, 'Come back', is all for my own sake. I never even raised the question whether such a return, if it were possible, would be good for her. I want her back as an ingredient in the restoration of *my* past. Could I have wished her anything worse? Having got once through death, to come back and then, at some later date, have all her dying to do over again? They call Stephen the first martyr. Hadn't Lazarus the rawer deal?
>
> I begin to see. My love for H. was of much the same quality as my faith in God. I won't exaggerate, though.

Whether there was anything but imagination in the faith, or anything but egoism in the love, God knows. I don't. There may have been a little more; especially in my love for H.[38]

Yet despite – or perhaps because of – his self-interrogation, no one could seriously doubt that Lewis loved his wife with a love that was deep and noble; that is obvious to anyone reading his book. Lewis himself no doubt thought – and not least because of his Christian faith – that his love would have been better had it been less egoistical. But this is not true, even if it is nonetheless true that his dissatisfaction with the egoism of his love was partly responsible for making it the inspiring and noble thing it was. The fact is that human love – the best kind of human love: real, full-blooded, profound and inspiring – is an egoistical thing; without that egoism it would not be the magnificent thing it is. The same may be said, as I have already suggested, for much else that we value in life.

This idea, roughly speaking, that moral goodness is held in place by something that that very goodness wishes to deny was obvious to La Rochefoucauld and others in the tradition of the great French *moralistes*, to Machiavelli, to Mandeville, to Nietzsche, to Adorno, to Auden and no doubt to others. But it is almost wholly ignored in the mainstream of moral philosophy, since there is, for example, as far as I know, no acknowledgement or serious discussion of the point I have made in the work of those philosophers in the mainstream who reflect on the nature of the virtues. For sure, virtue theorists often grant, indeed, wish to emphasize, as I have explored at some length, that the virtues benefit their possessor, and in that sense claim that there is a kind of egoism in being virtuous. But the thought that one gets something out of being virtuous is clearly not the same idea as the thought, which I am pressing, that the virtues are nourished by the vices (greed, envy, vanity, lust, hatred and so on) and that, therefore, the virtues and vices differ only in degree, that, as Nietzsche put the thought with respect to action, good deeds are sublimated evil ones and evil deeds coarse good ones.

There are no doubt many reasons for the lack of attention to the points I am making among those philosophers who reflect on the virtues. One is, I am sure, the inability to see clear-sightedly one's own love, and one's own desire for that which is good and decent, as being held in place by egoism, greed, vanity and the like. C. S. Lewis's love for his wife brings that out clearly: his egoistical need of her was central to his love, but he could not see things that way and, indeed, his not being able to see things this way was probably part of what made his love the fine thing it was. There is a kind of double-mindedness here in morality, a way in which we cannot see things steadily and at the same time see them as they really are. The case of Lewis provides an example of one form of this double-mindedness in the first-person, but there are second- and third-person forms too. For example, and as I mentioned earlier, when we educate children, we have good reason to be glad that our best efforts to make them completely morally good fail, since we know that various forms of envy, greed, vanity and the like stand one in good stead in life, stimulating people to much that is good and valuable. But we could never wish to encourage these characteristics in those we educate. I suspect that the truth is that, the self being what Freud said it was – that is, at origin, and always to a greater or lesser extent, antisocial, sexually aggressive and narcissistic – we have to do pretty much all we can to educate children to be morally good, since we shall never succeed wholly in eradicating these qualities from the soul. Yet we can be glad of this, since, as long as they do not become overwhelming, they stimulate life. If Iris Murdoch is right that 'our fantasies and reveries are not trivial and unimportant, they are profoundly connected with our energies and our ability to choose and act',[39] as I am sure she is, then if one were to get rid of these fantasies and reveries completely one would come to a stop. This is why Hannah Arendt made the point that perfect or pure goodness is destructive of the world.[40] The issue is not one of removing completely the egoism of the self, but of using it productively; it is not a matter of removing all fantasy and reverie, but of these becoming forces that are at the very least not inhibiting of the self and at best nurturing of its better possibilities.

A related though somewhat different way of thinking about the relation between virtue and egoism that I have been exploring – a way of thinking of it that clearly manifests the same spirit as my comments so far – was offered by Bernard Williams when he remarked: 'Nothing is more commonplace to us than that particular virtues not only coexist with, but carry with them, typical faults.'[41] We find examples of Williams's point everywhere: Wittgenstein's immense integrity carried with it a certain blindness to human frailty and weakness; William Hazlitt's impressive and vital energy was the very thing that led him often to be foolish, stubborn and unforgiving; Samuel Johnson's depth and insight brought with them much arrogance and the desire to dominate; Kafka's sensitivity rendered him incapable of certain ordinary forms of love; and so on. Of course, you could reply: this is all very well; things are like that, but they ought not to be and we ought to seek virtue that is not thus compromised (which is not the right word, as I have been arguing). But to respond in this way would be to miss the whole point of all that I am saying: human beings just are such that virtues bring with them weaknesses and vices. Not to accept that is not to accept that life of human beings, at least in part. Of course, one can wish to escape all that, and, as I have previously suggested, it is no doubt true that human beings cannot but long to be other than they are, to transcend themselves. It may even be that they would be much less impressive, including in their virtue, if they did not wish to be so much more than they are. As I have already said, it may not be possible to see reality both steadily and as it is – *and* that that makes up part of human greatness, as well as the tragedy of our condition.

Of course, working in the background to all these thoughts is the powerful influence of Christianity, which has always thought of moral goodness as utterly pure. For example, it is clear that Christianity conceptualizes true love as wholly free of any egoism. And Christianity has the example of Jesus, who symbolizes pure love – though Christianity itself, in my view, has nearly always fought shy of this and made its peace with the world too easily. Socrates had his version in the claim that the good man cannot be harmed, because the only thing that matters – matters to him and really matters in itself – is being virtuous. If you think that, then I doubt any argument will dislodge that belief. But you cannot just *say* you think it and then live in such a way as to show that you really think other things matter, like material comfort or success. That brings out that, in one sense, no one does believe it *literally*, because no one could seriously believe that, say, bodily health does not matter. If someone says he believes that virtue is the only thing that matters, then he must mean that it is the only thing that *really* matters, and then everything will turn on what he takes *really* to mean here. The point about Jesus' immensely impressive life is that he got about as close to not really caring about anything but goodness as one can, and ended up on the cross. I think that that is what you ought to expect if you are not naive and you really do try to believe that virtue is the only thing that really matters. Simone Weil, who is one of the very few individuals who have sought genuinely to live a Christ-like life, would certainly have agreed, and she was willing to be destroyed by it. But I do not think that Weil – or Jesus for that matter – was wholly selfless, had no vanity or envy or greed. Jesus might symbolize pure goodness, but his psychology, insofar as we can reconstruct it, was a messier business: he often displayed what one might describe as a kind of magnificent egoism, as in Mary's anointing of his feet with very costly nard (John 12:3–8). Even Jesus' goodness was held in place by much that that goodness denied.

We are beguiled by the image of Jesus or, more generally, by the idea of perfect goodness or virtue on account of something I pointed out earlier, namely, that only the good or virtuous person suffers from a bad conscience. We can tell ourselves that the perfectly virtuous person would never so suffer, since he or she would never do anything to cause such suffering. As I mentioned earlier, no such person could ever exist, but we are seduced by such an image because it allows us to preserve the idea that being morally good is a form of health. This is so because the guilty conscience is evidently unhealthy in the sense of being enervating and destructive of peace of mind. Nietzsche developed that thought into the idea that morality is a form of illness. Freud said something similar in his great essay 'Civilization and its Discontents', in which he stressed that the stability of modern mass society depends upon the renunciation of many of our deepest impulses and needs: he believed, rightly in my view, as mentioned, that the self remains forever largely driven by violent and antisocial needs, is resolutely egoistical and caught up in sexual impulses whose nature it does not fully grasp. The best we can hope for is to learn to control these impulses and to live with them in a reasonably adult manner. And that, indeed, shows us something else about the Aristotelian view discussed above: it supposes the forces of the self to be fairly amenable to moral education, not such as to resist such education and be at best subdued by it, as on Freud's view. For it is only if one is optimistic about the educability of the self that one can suppose it likely that one will find one's happiness in virtue, since only such optimism will allow one to suppose that the forces of the self can be taken up into virtue, be transformed by it and find their good in it. If, however, as Freud supposes, the self is always to a greater or lesser extent recalcitrant to moral education, then the best we can hope for is an uneasy compromise between virtue and whatever it wants to educate in the self. Freud would thus agree that morality is largely about renunciation, though necessary. Morality, which we do value deeply, and rightly so, is on this view a kind of nightmare. And in that gap between what we need and value, morality, and what morality actually is, we are faced by something central to our tragic condition. Philosophers are certainly not alone in wanting to avoid that tragedy by turning the nightmare into a dream.

* * *

I have been exploring our fractured relation to morality in modernity. But, of course, if we have such a fractured relation to morality one central reason for that is the Holocaust, which I discussed in part in Chapter Two and to which I return in ending this one.

Once again, the work of Hannah Arendt proves important here. One of the central reasons for this is that she witnessed at first hand the collapse of values brought about by the Nazis. She wrote:

> Among the many things which were still thought to be 'permanent and vital' at the beginning of the century and yet have not lasted [are] the moral issues . . . the few rules and standards according to which men used to tell right from wrong, and which were invoked to judge or justify others and themselves, and whose validity were [sic] supposed to be self-evident to every sane person either as a part of divine or of natural law.[42]

If it seems incredible to us that people could have had confidence in their values in the way that Arendt describes, then we must remember that this is precisely because of the collapse that she describes. Stefan Zweig, who, like Arendt, also witnessed the collapse in question, wrote a wonderful autobiography whose title, *The World of Yesterday*, refers to that, to the sense of the complete loss of a world – the world.

> *Before* this 'New Order', the murder of a single person without legal process and without apparent reason would have shocked the world; torture was considered unthinkable in the twentieth century . . . But *now* after repeated Bartholomew nights and all those people put to death through torture in the SA prisons and behind barbed wire, what did a single injustice or earthly suffering signify? In 1938, after Austria, our universe had become accustomed to inhumanity, to lawlessness, and brutality as never in centuries before. In a former day the occurrences in wretched Vienna alone would have been sufficient to cause international ostracism, but in 1938 the world conscience was silent or merely muttered before it forgot and forgave.[43]

Arendt says that it was

> as though morality suddenly stood revealed in the original meaning of the word, as a set of mores, customs and manners, which could be exchanged for another set with hardly more trouble than it would take to change the table manners of an individual or a people.[44]

Jean Améry, too, was haunted by the same thing:

> The intellectual . . . who experienced the logic of the SS as a reality that proved itself hour by hour, now took a few fateful steps further in his thinking. Were not those who were preparing to destroy him in the right, owing to the undeniable fact that they were the stronger ones? . . . Yes, the SS could carry on as it was: there are no natural

rights, and moral categories arise and pass like the fashions. A Germany was there that drove Jews and its political opponents to their death since it believed that only in this way could it fully realize itself. And so what? Greek civilization had been built on slavery and an Athenian army had wreaked havoc on the island of Melos as had the ss in Ukraine . . . That is the way history was and that is the way it is. One had fallen under its wheel and tipped one's cap when a murderer came along.[45]

Moreover, after the war all this was overturned once more and a new liberal order was proclaimed. It happened overnight. 'Hence', wrote Arendt, 'we must say that we witnessed the total collapse of a "moral" order not once but twice, and this sudden return to "normality" . . . can only reinforce our doubts'.[46]

It goes without saying that these thinkers are not in any sense approving of what happened. Rather, the point is that morality has now become for them utterly baffling. It is one thing to know in the form of, let us say, a piece of historical information or as material for intellectual reflection, that, for example, the Athenians committed acts of atrocity in Melos; it is quite another to experience this happening here and now with consummate ease. The mind and the spirit reel in the face of it and the individual experiences a sense of vertigo. And that can exist perfectly well along with the conviction that what is happening is a barbarity. Indeed, that is part of the sense of vertigo.

That, I think, is one of the crucial points at issue. The conviction that what the Nazis did was simply unspeakably brutal remains, yet somehow it coexists with the baffling sense of the utter contingency of having such a conviction, that it would take, or would have taken, so little for one to change one's view. There are those who respond to this by insisting that values are part of the fabric of the universe, to use a standard way of putting it, and others who draw the conclusion that moral relativism is true. In my view, both miss the point, for both positions are expressions of a longing for innocence, of a desire to be free of a kind of crippling self-consciousness that is, as Mill pointed out in a wonderful essay on Bentham, a kind of demon.[47] It is, I think, simply too late in the day to flee the tragic acknowledgement that our values, even though we are committed to them, are contingent and could have been otherwise. That is the price we pay for our historical consciousness, for our recognition that, however much we seek to give good reasons to justify our values, what we are doing is, in large part at least, seeking to give reasons for what we would believe anyway.

We believe, for example, in the equality of all human beings, but only yesterday John Locke, one of the Enlightenment architects of modern liberalism, would have thought that absurd. Moreover, human rights were always thought to depend on belief in God or to be self-evident. The u.s. Declaration of Independence reads: 'We hold these truths to be self-evident, that all men are created equal, that they are endowed by their Creator with certain unalienable Rights, that among these are Life, Liberty and the pursuit of Happiness.' Moreover, the UN Universal Declaration of Human Rights simply *asserts* that 'All human beings are born free and equal in dignity and rights'. It gives no reason for this claim at all. Both texts clearly take it to be self-evident that all human beings have human rights simply by virtue of being human. But this is not self-evident: it was not self-evident to Plato and Aristotle, for example. Even leaving aside the reference to the Christian God in the u.s. Declaration, they would have regarded such a claim as absurd. Of course, there are many philosophical attempts to justify human rights, and it is not possible here to explore these attempts in detail. None of them has been found to be wholly successful by those who have considered them. Be that as it may, it is helpful to look at the issue from the point of view of Arendt's criticism of the concept of human rights.

Thinking about those persons made stateless by the Nazi regime, she pointed out that it means nothing to say that they have human rights. This does not stop anyone treating them just as he wishes, and it does nothing to protect them. A stateless person is protected when he is accorded legal rights to protection by some state. But legal rights are not human rights, that is, rights that are supposed to attach to us simply by virtue of the fact that we are human beings. To say that someone has human rights is to miss the point; it helps no one until he is accorded legal rights. And to say that someone ought to possess legal rights because he possesses human rights does not help either. It is not as if insisting that someone has human rights means that any state is forced to accord him legal rights if it is not otherwise disposed to do this.

Simone Weil pointed this out too from another direction.[48] A young girl being forced into prostitution is not having her human rights violated, she said. Rather, *she* is being violated. And it is because *she* is being violated that we wish to accord her legal rights. If you say, 'Well, that is what I mean when I say that she has human rights', then the question is why you speak in this way rather than in the way Weil speaks. Why speak of human rights at all? And the answer is because we somehow assume that saying that someone has human rights has some kind of power over people to make them behave in a certain way. Arendt and Weil make the point that this is not true. Suppose a man to be torturing someone else. If you tell him that what he is doing is barbarous and cruel then he will probably continue. It would be naive in the extreme to suppose, however, that if one were to tell him that what he is doing violates the human rights of his victim then he would stop, as if that thought had some power over him that the thought that what he was doing was barbarous and cruel did not. The discourse of human rights has no power whatsoever over anyone who is not already disposed to think that the person in question ought to be treated with respect and dignity. And if a person or state is already disposed to treat someone in this way, he or it might express that view using the vocabulary of human rights. But that justifies nothing and has no power as such. Rather, it expresses what the person or state is disposed to believe anyway, namely, that the person in question ought to be treated with respect and dignity. It is that which would lead to someone or a state treating someone well or according him legal rights, if anything does. The discourse of human rights justifies nothing; rather, it expresses what we are disposed to believe anyway, in our liberal world view, namely, as the declarations say, that we are born free and equal and the like. That is why these declarations give no reason to justify belief in human rights, and that is why we take it to be self-evident that human beings have such rights. But that, as I say, just expresses what *we* think, which would have been thought absurd in most epochs of human history and is still thought absurd in some parts of the world today.

The truth, as it seems to me, is this: we believe that our liberal values are the true or correct values, but we also know that they are the contingent upshot of history, that things could have been quite otherwise and that we might have accepted quite different values, believing them to be true. In that sense, our values do indeed seem like customs, manners, with as little to justify them as there is to justify customs and manners – nothing much beyond 'this is the way we happen to do things.' When Sartre remarked: 'Tomorrow, after my death, some men may decide to establish Fascism, and the others may be so cowardly or so slack as to let them do so. If so, Fascism will then be the truth of man, and so much the worse for us',[49] he can be understood to be seeking to face this tragic reality. The awful truth is that this could happen, as it happened in Weimar Germany, where most people were just utterly ordinary individuals like you and me. Sartre's philosophy presents us with a tragic vision of human beings and, in my view, the aspect of it that we are discussing captures that perfectly. He is, I think, absolutely right that this expresses our forlorn condition, and that this engenders anxiety and despair in us. Our relation to our values is filled with uncertainty and unclarity, in the way I have sought to describe: we believe them, think they are the true values, yet know them to be contingent, to be like manners, in the sense that they are expressions of the way that we happen to do things, and that we might easily have accepted other values, believing them to be true and seeking to give reasons for them. We live in the cleft created by this profound tension. That is the lesson of Améry, Zweig, Arendt and others. We do them, and ourselves, a profound disservice, I believe, if we avert our eyes from their tragic insight.

FIVE

Among the Ruins

Ours, I have been arguing, is a tragic age. We are living in the ruins. 'The whole earth is our hospital / Endowed by the ruined millionaire', as T. S. Eliot has it in 'East Coker'. In previous chapters I have tried to explore some aspects of how this is so. Our homelessness is not something that Christianity ignored. On the contrary, it knew it well and sought to offer a reply to it. Christianity knows that we are born to suffer, that here, in this world, virtue is not rewarded with happiness and that the wicked often flourish; that we are mysterious to ourselves, are driven by forces we cannot understand and largely exposed in life to contingency and chance. But it says there is redemption for this, in God's love for us and knowledge of us and in Jesus' death on the cross. What the sceptical modern consciousness says is no, this is not so; there is no such redemption.

If our condition is tragic in the way I have been suggesting, then it would not be surprising if we were faced by what Nietzsche calls a great spiritual depression in culture. And, indeed, the intellectual history of the nineteenth and twentieth centuries is characterized by a central stream of cultural critical material which suggests that that is just the situation in modernity. Kierkegaard, for example, saw modernity as the realm of the cheap and shallow: 'Not only in the commercial world but in the realm of ideas as well, our age is holding a veritable clearance sale. Everything is had so dirt cheap that it is doubtful whether in the end anyone will bid.'[1] In this he anticipated Nietzsche, who believed that modernity was the triumph of what he called 'the last man', the kind of person who cares about nothing but his comfort and security and has lost all sense of anything deeper or more sustaining in life. Spengler's *Decline of the West* analyses the whole topic of the collapse of the West in extreme detail, claiming that the rich culture of the West has given way to the sterility of what he calls mere 'civilization'. Max Weber, meanwhile, as previously mentioned, speaks of the disenchantment of the West, in which we are subject to bureaucratic rationality that operates in wholly utilitarian terms, deprived of any sense of the sacred. Heidegger sees most of us as hopelessly sunk in inauthentic lives and Sartre claims that bad faith is unavoidable. Then there is Camus, for whom the human condition in modernity is tragic because it is absurd: between what we need and want in life and the inability of the world to give us that, we live as in an abyss, struck by the absurdity of our condition and our precarious place in existence.

Hannah Arendt, on the other hand, looking back nostalgically at the Greeks, laments the collapse of the idea that human beings find their true fulfilment in the public sphere of politics and prefer to cultivate their private interests. Adorno, meanwhile, largely agrees with Weber's analysis of our subjection to a certain desiccating kind of reason, while adding that various patterns of domination and control typical of Nazism are still present in modernity, which is thus a kind of mirror of fascism. He is not alone in thinking that Nazism was in many ways a bourgeois phenomenon and makes us see what we really are. More recently the Italian linguist and cultural critic Raffaele Simone, drawing on Tocqueville, has argued that we have abdicated serious engagement in political life and turned ourselves over to being dominated by what he calls 'the gentle monster': our political masters and their cronies keep us acquiescent by turning the public space into an arena of spectacle, fun and entertainment, and, because we enjoy this mindless slavery, we are complicit in the whole thing. Other thinkers see us as living in an age of sentimentality, a world in which we are rapidly turning as much as possible into kitsch and creating even more of it from scratch. Others see us as having capitulated more or less entirely to the mercantile values of the marketplace, in which all of us are consumers and nothing has any value but what can be bought and sold. And still others think that we are living in what Christopher Lasch called a culture of narcissism, though Lasch meant that the narcissistic personality has a weak sense of self – the title of his later *The Minimal Self* makes the point. Others agree with him about the narcissism of contemporary life, but think of it more in terms of hedonistic egoism.

Between them these thinkers and others who share the same bleak outlook on modern culture surely capture something of our zeitgeist, even if one might disagree with some of the details. I use the term 'zeitgeist' advisedly: we are speaking here of the spirit of the times, and it is quite consistent with that to think that there are things in modernity to appreciate and value. A culture is pervaded by a certain spirit, just as a relationship or a team or an organization can be, and in all these cases the spirit cannot be reduced to individual persons from whose interaction it emerges and whose interaction it influences. Anyone who thinks that our age is tragic for the reasons I have tried to articulate in this book will be likely to think that the spirit of the times is, indeed, bleak. He will probably agree with D. H. Lawrence, writing in the aftermath of the First World War:

> Ours is essentially a tragic age, so we refuse to take it tragically. The cataclysm has happened, we are among the ruins, we start to build up new little habitats, to have new little hopes. It is rather hard work: there is now no

smooth road into the future: but we go round, or scramble over the obstacles. We've got to live, no matter how many skies have fallen.[2]

In one sense, perhaps, most people do not, indeed, take the tragedy of the age seriously; they would not, perhaps, see it as I have described it in this book, for example. But that is not to say that they avoid it: it is there in their suffering and in their failure, which they must face without the support of religion. We all need to do what Lawrence describes as our task: 'build up new little habitats, to have new little hopes . . . We've got to live'. Perhaps we see this best in our therapeutic culture, one of the deepest features of modernity, which very largely makes sense to us only because in various ways it knows of the tragedy of the age.

It would, of course, be consoling if one were able to believe that there are some clear ways in which we can confront the sense of the tragedy of life and find in the ruins clear reasons to affirm life. Indeed, because this would be so profoundly consoling there is a strong temptation here, as in many other aspects of life, to say what one *thinks one thinks*, or, perhaps better, what one would *like* to think, rather than what one *really* thinks. Nietzsche's published writings are full of affirmations of existence that are belied in various ways by his private notes, letters and the like. Those affirmations of life are not lies. But they were attempts on Nietzsche's part to get himself to believe something that he was not at all sure he really believed. His affirmative view vied with a negative view that always lay in wait for him, and he struggled not to give into it. There is something noble and moving in that attitude. But, in truth, in some deep way he was more inclined to think life tragic in some finally destructive manner, and anyone who reads his work without that recognition in mind is likely to miss a great deal of the strength, nobility and depth of his philosophy.

Be that as it may, it must be emphasized, that, so far as consolation for our tragic condition goes, there are some forms of suffering, failure and confusion that are so deep that there is not the slightest chance of the person who experiences them doing anything more than simply bearing them – and even that may be beyond him; he might simply be destroyed by them. In such cases it would be indecent to suggest that there is some way in which the person in question can, after all, transcend the tragedy that is, or is endemic to, his life. Nietzsche said that without music life would be a mistake, and I often share this sense of things. But to suppose that someone like Jean Améry, nursing his resentment and total collapse of faith in the human world having been tortured, should or could find in music a response to his suffering would be to fail to understand him and to offer him a profound affront at the same time.

Further, it seems to me necessary to acknowledge that, if one is able to look the tragedy of existence squarely in the face and find things in life that make it nonetheless worthwhile, then this is largely a matter of luck. The luck is partly what philosophers call 'constitutive luck', the kind of luck that one has simply to be such-and-such a person with such-and-such dispositions of temperament, sensibility and the like. It is also a matter of luck at a more local level, the luck one has in terms of the people one meets, the place where one lives and so on.

But there are some who refuse to accommodate themselves to the tragedy of existence, those, we might say, whose luck leads them to an incapacity, an unwillingness, to make the necessary concessions. There are, for example, some thinkers, such as Améry, but also the Russian Lev Shestov and the Franco-Romanian Emil Cioran, whose thinking is characterized by a relentless rejection of, indeed, rage against, any suggestion that the task of philosophy is to help us to accommodate ourselves better to the tragedy of life. They offer no system, no consolation, no answers, seeing philosophy's true vocation in the relentless explosion of alleged certainties, the continued raising of inconvenient questions, the tireless exposure of all that makes us claim we know when we do not.

Shestov, it is true, accepted some version of Christianity, but it does not stop his work from being filled with a kind of rage against the tragedy of existence. Améry, for his part, said that he had lost all faith in human beings and the world, and his work radiates a hard, bitter resentment. And Cioran's work is likewise characterized by a rage, misery and horror at existence that makes reading him weirdly exhilarating and at the same time a relentlessly miserable activity. One of his books is entitled *The Trouble with Being Born*, which pretty much sums it all up. And, although he comes from another epoch altogether, Cioran would have agreed with La Rochefoucauld: 'Philosophy triumphs easily over evils past and evils to come. But present evils triumph over philosophy.'[3]

The point is well made in Johnson's *Rasselas*. At one point, Rasselas finds what he takes to be a happy and wise man. In Chapter Eighteen we read that this man 'discoursed with great energy on the government of the passions' and recommended a tranquil acceptance of the world, governed by reason in all things. A person thus governed 'is no longer the slave of fear nor the fool of hope; is no more emaciated by envy, inflamed by anger, emasculated by tenderness, or depressed by grief; but walks on calmly through the tumults or privacies of life'. Rasselas is immensely impressed by this man, and tells his friend Imlac of him, who replies magnificently: 'Be not too hasty to trust or to admire the teachers of morality: they discourse like angels, but they live like men.'

Imlac is right. A few days later Rasselas finds the wise man broken and wretched: his daughter has died. Rasselas reminds him of his discourses:

'Have you then forgot the precepts,' said Rasselas, 'which you so powerfully enforced? Has wisdom no strength to arm the heart against calamity? Consider that external things are naturally variable, but truth and reason are always the same.' 'What comfort,' said the mourner, 'can truth and reason afford me? Of what effect are they now, but to tell me that my daughter will not be restored?'

The Prince, whose humanity would not suffer him to insult misery with reproof, went away, convinced of the emptiness of rhetorical sounds, and the inefficacy of polished periods and studied sentences.[4]

That the philosopher is a stoic is of less importance than the fact that Johnson is clearly intent on showing that philosophy is largely impotent in the face of life's pain and suffering. But there is no animus in this passage, which is one of its marvels. Indeed, there is, in my view, in Johnson's thinking here, a humanity, a generosity, an understanding of and honesty in the face of the human condition that moral philosophy often sorely lacks.

Yet perhaps philosophy is not always and everywhere as impotent as it is in the case of Johnson's stoic. I once asked a psychoanalyst friend of mine what all the years of her own analysis had given her, how they had changed her. She said that she felt she could not say exactly what it was, but that it was probably something very small, but very important, something that had changed her in ways she could not fully articulate. That struck me as wise. And I think that years of reading philosophy – or literature or history or sociology or the like – might have the same effect. As Nietzsche says in *Daybreak*:

Small doses – If a change is to be as deep as possible, one must apply the remedy in the smallest doses, but unceasingly for long periods. What great thing can be created all at once? We must, therefore, guard against exchanging violently and precipitately the moral conditions with which we are familiar for a new valuation of things, – indeed, we may even wish to continue living in the old way for a long time, until probably at some very distant period we become aware of the fact that *the new valuation* has made itself the dominant power within us, and that its small doses to which we must from now on become accustomed have set up a new nature within us.[5]

Small doses over a long time may help. A little, I think, but not much. They may help with the lesser pains of life, so long as those pains are not prolonged, but I am not sure they can help much with the greater pains that confront us. And if they can help it will also be a matter of luck that you are the kind of person whom they can help. In a way, the rage of someone like Cioran is a rage against philosophy's claim to be able to deliver more than it can, a rage at its optimism or dishonesty and a rage against those philosophers who tell us what they think – like Johnson's stoic – when in reality it is actually only what they think they think.

Some people, of course, pin their hopes on moral progress. We saw something of this in the previous chapter. That the world is in some ways a morally better place than it was previously is no doubt true. But that is hardly the point. Those who believe in moral progress believe not just that, but usually that this progress will go on inevitably. Witness Richard Dawkins who, in speaking of the growth of liberal values, writes that most of us in the twenty-first century are

way ahead of our counterparts in the Middle Ages, or in the time of Abraham, or even as recently as the 1920s. The whole wave keeps moving, and even the vanguard of an earlier century . . . would find itself well behind the laggers of a later century . . . Over the longer timescale, the progressive trend is unmistakable and will continue.[6]

He has no way of knowing it will continue. It is just an article of faith. Moreover, he seems to have forgotten the horrors of the trenches of the Great War and of Auschwitz. Be that as it may, if there is one thing we know about recent history it is that those who committed the atrocities of the Holocaust were in many ways just like us, normal people, not especially wicked, but weak and fearful as we all are in various ways. There is no guarantee at all that moral progress will continue. It is not cumulative and can be lost overnight. And the central reason for this is that, as I argued in Chapter One, human beings are creatures who are deeply in conflict with themselves: such creatures can never attain the stability necessary for moral progress to be guaranteed. As Freud pointed out, civilization and barbarism are both natural to human beings and in many ways feed from each other. Moreover, in times of economic hardship, when resources are scarce, human beings' raw egoism shows itself almost immediately. Stand on the platform of a busy London train terminal at rush hour and watch the way in which naked self-interest asserts itself unthinkingly in those waiting as they crowd towards the doors of the train as it pulls in, aware that there are more passengers than seats, and you will see the point. The reason that we in the West live in a less violent world has largely to do with the fact that, as wealth spreads, there is less reason to behave with aggression towards others to get what they have and more to lose if one does and the attempt fails. I doubt very much that sensitive liberal respect for others' property would last long in a world of food and water shortages.

Why not, then, just give oneself up to the rage of someone like Cioran, perhaps ameliorated a little with some 'small doses'? Should we just refuse an accommodation with the tragedy of life?

Not long after Améry committed suicide in 1978, Levi wrote in his reflections on him that, though he much admired

Améry's taking up of the cudgels against the world, his bitterness had

> brought him to positions of such severity and intransigence as to make him incapable of finding joy in life, even of living: whoever 'takes up arms' against the whole world finds his dignity again, but pays an extremely high price for that, for it is sure that he will be defeated.[7]

Levi is surely right: there is something thoroughly admirable in those who look the tragedy of life in the eyes and refuse the false consolations, the self-deceptions, the cravenness that keep the rest of us going. But he is also right that the price to pay is high – very high.

Nietzsche expressed one of the central problems here in suggesting that untruth is the condition of life, as I have previously mentioned in speaking of his view concerning the ubiquity of illusion in life. He did not mean, of course, that one can just will oneself to believe something to be true when one believes it to be false because believing it would make one's life better. He meant, rather, that we all believe things that are in fact false, although they seem true to us, and believing them helps us make sense of life and avoid its tragedy. But, although it is true that one cannot just decide what to believe, it remains the case that one can decide not to think about things too much and thus come to accept convenient but false views. Allowing oneself to be distracted is what is at issue, and we all do this, at least to some extent. Camus recommends a bitter affirmation of the reality of one's tragic condition, an affirmation that allows one to live. We must learn, he thinks, to embrace the pain and contradictions of the human condition without self-deception. This is a kind of rebellion or revolt. But the problem is how to do this. Cioran would say that the pain and contradictions *cannot* be affirmed and, if you think otherwise, it is because you do not know them as they really are.

There is clearly a kind of standoff here insofar as any possible affirmation would be suspect for Cioran – not a full affirmation of the tragedy of existence, but some kind of evasion of it after all. No doubt this is partly why Camus said that the first philosophical problem was that of suicide. For what he wanted to say was that a full recognition of the tragedy of existence would involve a temptation to suicide, so that the question was whether one could have the former without the latter. It seems, surely, somehow to miss the point if one insists that anyone who does not kill himself *ipso facto* has not tasted the full bitterness of life's tragedy. Apart from the fact that Cioran did not kill himself, there simply must be room – spiritual and intellectual room – for Camus' possibility.

I think what this helps us see is that we are looking at the problem from the wrong end. There cannot, I think, be some general answer to the question of whether it is possible to accept the tragedy of life without self-deception and yet find life worth living. There can only be an answer for each person, a first-person answer. That does not rule out, of course, the possibility that one could think that a given person's answer is open to criticism or rejection. I once read in the newspaper about a man who, during a storm, went up onto the roof of his house to secure the chimney and tiles. He was struck by lightning and lost both arms and legs. He had managed to make a new life for himself and find things worth living for. In an interview he said that every person has his or her own suffering and the right to it. That was a sign of his generosity of spirit, perhaps something he had in fact learned through his own suffering. It helps give us a sense of the reality of what he had experienced and the reality of his tragedy. Nonetheless, it is consistent with seeing why his suffering led him to speak as he did of others' pain to disagree with his estimation of their situation. Indeed, the journalist conducting the interview did disagree and surely was right to do so. A given person may think that his suffering is deep and has given him insight into the tragedy of life, but we might judge that this is self-indulgence or self-pity because the suffering, by comparison with that of others, was not really so profound. Such judgements are contentious and open to discussion, but they are surely possible. Nonetheless, to ask, for example, which of two individuals has suffered the more and thus has truly descended to the depths of tragedy is often both pointless and unseemly. Van Gogh's life was miserable in many ways, and so was that of Dostoevsky. That, in a way, is all there is to be said. That life was tragic for both of them seems to me, at any rate, clear, but it also seems clear to me that they both managed to live beyond and through that tragedy in its full bitterness. I am sure that Cioran would agree.

If the issue here is one of a first-person response to tragedy, to its affirmation, then different people will have different possibilities for finding such affirmation. So, although it might be that for some given person finding solace in, say, the magnificence of the natural world, as Camus recommends, has nothing to offer for his suffering, it is far from obvious that it has nothing to offer to anyone. For sure, it cannot be the whole answer, but, says Camus, if there is no life after this, if this is all we have got, then either we affirm that, or there is nothing:

> In a moment, when I throw myself down among the absinthe plants to allow their scent to enter into my body, I shall be aware, contrary to all preconceptions, of accomplishing a truth which is that of the sun as well as of my death. In a sense, it really is my life that I am gambling here, a life suffused with the taste of warm stone, full of the sighs of the sea and the cicadas that are now beginning to sing. The breeze is cool and the sky blue. I love this life with abandon, and want to speak of

it freely: it makes me proud of my human condition. Nonetheless, people have often said to me: there is nothing here to be proud of. But there is: this sun, this sea, my heart leaping with youth, my body which tastes of salt and the immense surroundings where tenderness and glory meet in the yellow and the blue. It is in order to conquer this that I apply my energy and my resources. Everything here leaves me intact, I lose nothing of myself, I put on no mask: it is enough for me patiently to learn the difficult task of living, which demands all their art.[8]

The magnificence of this evocation of worldly physicality is not to be dismissed lightly.

Crucial here, in any case, is that any person must be prepared to leave open the question of whether what he took to be an affirmation of the tragedy of life was not, after all, something else – perhaps a form of self-aggrandizement. One needs to know that what one takes to be such affirmation might turn to ash. This is just what Johnson's stoic did not know: he thought that he had the answer, that he was invulnerable, that he had left his weakness behind him for good. This is a profound error, not made any better by the fact that it happens all the time, complacency being one of human beings' most striking characteristics. What this helps us see is that, beyond the question of *what* one believes, there is an issue of *how* one believes it, the *manner* in which one believes it. This is no doubt one of the reasons why Cioran was relentlessly critical of the dogmatism that seems inherent in human beings and repeated his cry for an honest scepticism. Johnson's stoic was not at all sceptical, and did not leave his view open to possible failure or repudiation. He might have been able to hold it in a much more tentative fashion, and making fewer demands on it might have allowed it to give him more, but this requires, I think, intense spiritual discipline.

There remains something terribly important about those, such as Cioran, Améry and Shestov, who resolutely refuse to make their peace with the tragedy of life. In the Introduction of this book I suggested that philosophy and tragedy were inevitable antagonists. In their refusal to claim that philosophy can help us accommodate ourselves to tragedy, these philosophers express the same idea from a different, but complementary, point of view. For they say: it is not just that philosophy cannot understand tragedy; it cannot help us live with it. But that is, I think, because they supposed that any philosophy that could claim to do such would have to be a systematic philosophy that falsified reality. Moreover, they supposed that anyone committed to such a system would have to believe that he had found an invulnerable truth. But philosophy need not be systematic: the aphoristic and essayist writings of these philosophers show that, after all, there are other possibilities, though they are certainly right that such a type of philosophy remains marginal to the mainstream, and none of them is anywhere near the centre of the discipline as it is now understood. Moreover, however unusual their type of philosophy might have been, there can be little doubt that it did help them make sense of the tragedy of life, if only in the expression of a kind of highly articulate rage.

In any case, philosophy is, obviously enough, only one way of seeking to accept the tragedy of life – or refusing to do so, raging against it. Aside from all the other ways in art and literature, there remains the fact that different individuals' responses might find no articulation other than in their life. Thoreau remarked that the 'mass of men lead lives of quiet desperation'.[9] We could read this simply as falsifiable generalization about human beings. But it is probably better to read it as an expression of pity for the fact that human beings suffer so much, however that might be, and that we each in our own way have to find ways of living with, accepting or affirming that – or raging against it. That is, Thoreau is inviting us into a sense of solidarity with others, a compassionate recognition of our general plight. From such a point of view we are being asked not simply to acknowledge the tragic nature of life, but also to be as non-judgemental as possible concerning our evasions and deceptions in the face of it. We are all seeking to make the best of a bad job.

In his memoir *The Summing Up*, W. Somerset Maugham writes of someone whom he calls Brown:

> He was twenty-six . . . He had a little money, enough to live on in those inexpensive days, and . . . made up his mind to devote himself to literature . . . I knew him till his death forty years later. For twenty years he amused himself with thinking what he would write when he really got down to it, and for another twenty with what he could have written if the fates had been kinder . . . He was completely devoid of willpower. He was senti-mental and vain . . . As an old man, after a life of complete indolence, bald and emaciated, he had an ascetic air so that you might have taken him for a don who had spent long years in ardent and disinterested research. The spirituality of his expression suggested the tired scepticism of a philosopher who had plumbed the secrets of existence and discovered nothing but vanity. Having gradually wasted his small fortune, he preferred to live on the generosity of others rather than work . . . His self-complacency never deserted him . . . I do not think he ever had an inkling that he was an out-rageous sham. His whole life was a lie, but . . . I am convinced he would have looked upon it as well spent.[10]

This man Brown, it seems, never confronted the tragedy of life, for he did not know of it. His self-deception protected him from that. Yet, in a way, his whole life was tragic. At least it seems to me that a life is tragic if it is a sham, a lie. It is an image of waste. If most of us avoid the tragedy of life through stratagems of self-deception and distraction, then we risk ending up in the tragedy of a person like Brown. This is why, as I mentioned in an earlier chapter, Dostoevsky said that he was fearful of nothing so much as being unworthy of his suffering. He meant, among other things, that not to be worthy of it would be to avoid facing it through self-deception and complacency, and that that would be an even greater tragedy than the suffering itself.

If we are to make something of our life then we need to find some kind of place, not too indecorous, between an honest recognition of the tragedy of our suffering, failure, confusion and homelessness on the one hand, and the tragedy of living a lie on the other. That is in a way obvious, even banal, and has been said countless times in different ways. It is worth saying again only because it reminds us that it is in the finding of such a place that we manifest our humanity, for seeking such a place is definitive of what our humanity is. It is, in a way, *the* task of human beings, and it is central to our moral lives.

SIX

Some Final Thoughts

In his poem 'Church Going', Philip Larkin, speaking of the church, writes: 'A serious house on serious earth it is/ In whose blent air all our compulsions meet/ Are recognised, and robed as destinies.'[1] These deeply moving lines capture supremely the sense of disenchantment so characteristic of modernity that I mentioned at the outset of this book. What Christianity did was, indeed, to dignify our compulsions.

Consider, for example, the fact that we all of us, sooner or later, arrive at the recognition that our lives are hopelessly compromised in various ways: through our sufferings and those we have inflicted, through our folly, through our waste. We all need forgiveness. Christianity dignifies our folly and offers that forgiveness. It does this by placing the compromise of our lives in the structure of the story of the Fall, channelling our otherwise chaotic failings into the order of a narrative, making sense of it in the parables and stories of the New Testament and the Hebrew Bible, and offering forgiveness and redemption through the story of Christ's Passion. Without that, we are just left with the bare fact: our folly and sufferings, of which we have to try and make sense without any of what Christianity offers. Or think about our experience of sexual desire, which Christianity offers to transform from a hungry urge of the self into the expression of a sacred longing.

None of that is to deny the absurdities, corruption and oppressive moralizing that has so often attended Christianity.

It is simply to say that, despite all that, the better possibilities of Christianity have offered something whose absence leaves us facing ourselves as creatures full of naked compulsions. For example, Freud, whatever else we think about this description, expresses a sense of such compulsions when he describes the normal sexual aim in adults 'as being the union of the genitals in the act known as copulation, which leads to a release of the sexual tension and a temporary extinction of the sexual instinct'.[2] It is not so much that Freud is wrong; it is rather that this description of the expression of sexual desire is aggressively free of any sense of mystery or wonder and totally indifferent to the possible connection of sex with love. It is, indeed, a description of sex as totally disenchanted.

Of course, not everyone would see anything problematic in that or think that without Christianity there is any great absence. Plenty of people do not feel the loss of which I am speaking. Moreover, we all get by using various cultural fragments that allow us to keep going when faced with the stark reality of, for example, our sexual desires, investing them with the hope that they can be 'robed' in the garb of, perhaps, romantic love – though our increasingly 'pornographized' culture suggests that plenty of people have given up the attempt. For two thousand years Christianity had the monopoly on transforming us from merely failed animals into noble but flawed human beings, but other traditions have also been available and it is to these that many resort now, knowingly or otherwise, to try to take up the slack: bits and pieces left over from the Greeks and Romans, Renaissance humanism, Enlightenment reason, Romanticism and so on – but mainly Romanticism. Buddhism, too, is increasingly important in the modern West in this context. I do not mean that none of these traditions can help. They certainly can, and some of them are noble and inspiring. But my point is that these are private projects of individuals, as Yeats has it: 'the centre cannot hold' – with the loss of Christianity we have lost the overarching vision of the world that for so long people defined themselves in terms of, or against. Now many are, as I have said, just indifferent to it.

But for those who do feel that the loss of Christianity matters, Larkin captures movingly what is at issue. I myself feel deeply torn: on the one hand, the decay of Christianity seems to me to be, in many ways, a cultural disaster, for reasons that I have tried to make clear in this book. But sometimes I do not feel this way, feeling, rather, liberated, light of spirit. In this I identify myself very strongly with Nietzsche, who possessed what Erich Heller called a 'dis-inherited mind', but who was also able to feel set free by the decay of Christianity. He was unlike the two other most influential thinkers of the nineteenth century, Marx and Freud, neither of whom, for all their genius, had any real feeling for religion at all.

The disenchanted world is a world in which meaning is at best elusive and often absent. That is central to the tragedy of modernity that I have traced in various ways in this book. But that problem about meaning pretty much presupposes that what D. H. Lawrence called 'the bread-and-butter problems of alimentation' have been solved for the individuals in question. For many, they have not been. That, I believe, contrary to those who think that tragedy is only to be found in the theatre, is also tragic. We are reminded of these two sides to the issue by something Simone de Beauvoir says in her autobiography. She speaks of a meeting with Simone Weil:

> She intrigued me because of her great reputation for intelligence and her bizarre getup . . . I don't know how the conversation got going. She said sharply that only one thing in the world mattered these days: the revolution that would provide enough food for the whole world. I retorted, in no less a peremptory fashion, that the problem was not to ensure human beings' happiness, but that

they find a meaning in their existence. She looked me up and down and said, 'It's clear you've never gone hungry.' Our relations ended right there.[3]

We live in a world in which well over 800 million people do not have enough to eat. But there is enough food to feed them. Owing to the idiocies of how we organize our life, they are hungry. That, in my view, is clearly tragic. But it is tragic too when people find their lives meaningless. Weil is right: she speaks for the poor and destitute. Beauvoir is right: she speaks for the spiritually lost and confused. They both remind us of human beings' tragic vulnerability as the desperately needy creatures we are.

REFERENCES

All translations from other languages into English are mine, unless indicated otherwise.

Preface

1 Rush Rhees, *On Religion and Philosophy*, ed. D. Z. Phillips (Cambridge, 1997), p. 150.

Introduction: Philosophy and Tragedy: A Personal View

1 Sándor Márai, *The Rebels*, trans. George Szirtes (New York, 2007), p. 36.
2 Jorge Luis Borges, 'Borges y yo' [1960], in *Narraciones* (Barcelona, 1982), pp. 155–6.
3 Quoted in Margaret Mills Harper, 'Yeats and the Occult', in *The Cambridge Companion to W. B. Yeats*, ed. Marjorie Howes and John Kelly (Cambridge, 2006), p. 144.
4 Miguel de Unamuno, *Del sentimiento trágico de la vida* [1913] (Madrid, 2013), p. 28.
5 Iris Murdoch, *The Sovereignty of Good* (London, 1985), p. 71.
6 Michael McGhee, *Transformations of Mind: Philosophy as Spiritual Practice* (Cambridge, 2000), p. 8.
7 Robert Nozick, *Philosophical Explanations* (Cambridge, MA, 1981), pp. 2–3.
8 Cf. George Lakoff and Mark Johnson, *Metaphors We Live By* (Chicago, IL, 2003), pp. 4ff.
9 Nozick, *Philosophical Explanations*, p. 4.
10 Ibid.
11 Arieh Sachs, 'Samuel Johnson on "The Vacuity of Life"', *Studies*

in English Literature, 1500–1900, III/3 (Summer 1963), p. 357.

12 Robert Nozick, *Anarchy, State, and Utopia* (Oxford, 1974), p. xii.

13 Nozick, *Philosophical Explanations*, p. 8.

14 Martha Nussbaum, *The Fragility of Goodness* (Cambridge, 1986), p. xliii.

15 William James, 'The Present Dilemma in Philosophy', in *Pragmatism and Other Writings* (Harmondsworth, 2000), p. 7.

16 Philip Larkin, 'An Interview with John Haffenden', in *Further Requirements: Interviews, Broadcasts, Statements and Reviews, 1952–1985*, ed. Anthony Thwaite (London, 2002), pp. 49–53.

17 P. F. Strawson, 'Social Morality and Individual Ideal', in *Freedom and Resentment and Other Essays* (London, 1974), p. 29.

18 One of the few who have made it is Mary Midgley. See her *Science and Poetry* (London, 2001), p. 39.

19 James, 'The Present Dilemma in Philosophy', pp. 8–9.

20 Virginia Woolf, *The Waves* [1931] (Oxford, 2008), pp. 53, 54, 67, 30, 44.

21 Kathleen Raine, *Autobiographies* (London, 1991), p. 263.

22 Georg Lukács, *Soul and Form*, trans. Anna Bostock (London, 1980), p. 153.

23 Theodor Adorno, *Minima Moralia* [1951], trans. E.F.N. Jephcott (London, 1987), §44.

ONE Ontology

1 Sophocles, 'Oedipus at Colonus', in *The Theban Plays* [c. 401 BC], trans. E. F. Watling (Harmondsworth, 1983), ll. 1261–8.

2 George Orwell, 'Benefit of Clergy: Some Notes on Salvador Dalí', in *The Penguin Essays of George Orwell* (Harmondsworth, 1984), p. 254.

3 T. S. Eliot, *The Cocktail Party* [1949] (London, 1982), Act II, p. 124.

4 John Calder, *The Philosophy of Samuel Beckett* (London, 2001), p. 51.

5 Samuel Johnson, *The History of Rasselas, Prince of Abissinia* [1759], ed. D. J. Enright (Harmondsworth, 1985).

6 Ibid., pp. 41–2.

7 Ibid., p. 45.

8 Simon Critchley, 'Phaedra's Malaise', in *Rethinking Tragedy*, ed. Rita Felski (Baltimore, MD, 2008), p. 193.

9 Terry Eagleton, 'Commentary', in *Rethinking Tragedy*, ed. Felski, p. 339.

10 Gabriel Josipovici, *Contre-Jour* (Manchester, 1986), pp. 42–3.

11 Primo Levi, 'Jean Améry, il filosofo suicida', in *L'asimmetria e la vita: articoli e saggi 1955–1987*, ed. M. Belpoliti (Torino, 2002), p. 70.

12 F. Scott Fitzgerald, *The Great Gatsby* [1925], ed. Tony Tanner (Harmondsworth, 2000).

13 Ibid., p. 115.

14 Ibid., p. 125.

15 Ibid., p. 106.

16 Ibid.

17 Ibid., p. 171.

18 Ibid., p. lvi.

19 Cf. Joshua Foa Dienstag, *Pessimism* (Princeton, NJ, 2006), esp. pp. 19–25.

20 Italo Svevo, *La coscienza di Zeno* [1923] (Milan, 2011).

21 Charles Baudelaire, 'Anywhere out of the World: N'importe où hors du monde', in *Le Spleen de Paris: Petits poèmes en prose* [1869] (Paris, 2003), p. 205.

22 Svevo, *La coscienza di Zeno*, p. 151.

23 Ibid., p. 172.

24 Ibid., p. 131.

25 Ibid.

26 Ibid.

27 Ibid., p. 132.

28 Erich Heller, *Kafka* (London, 1977), pp. 113–14.

TWO Pollution

1 Robert Nozick, 'The Holocaust', in *The Examined Life: Philosophical Meditations* (New York, 1990), pp. 236–42.

2 Primo Levi, *I sommersi e i salvati* [1986] (Torino, 2003), pp. 66–7.

3 Susan Neiman, *Evil in Modern Thought: An Alternative History of Philosophy* (Princeton, NJ, 2002), p. 256. Cf. the essays in *Echoes from the Holocaust: Philosophical Reflections in a Dark Time*, ed. Alan Rosenberg and Gerald E. Meyers (Philadelphia, PA, 1988), many of which grapple with just this problem.

4 Levi, *I sommersi e i salvati*, p. 55.

5 Auden's notes to *New Year Letter*, quoted in Gabriel Josipovici, *Touch* (New Haven, CT, 1996), p. 37.

6 Theodor Adorno, *Minima Moralia* [1951], trans. E.F.N. Jephcott (London, 1987), §18.

7 Neiman, *Evil in Modern Thought*, p. 305.

8 Raymond Williams, *Modern Tragedy* [1966] (Ontario, 2006), p. 195.

THREE Suffering

1 A. C. Bradley, 'Hegel's Theory of Tragedy', in *Oxford Lectures on Poetry* [1909] (New York, 1999), p. 82.

2 George Steiner, *The Death of Tragedy* [1961] (Yale, CT, 1996), p. 10.

3 W. H. Auden, *Lectures on Shakespeare* (Princeton, NJ, 2000), p. 255.

4 Ibid., p. 204.

5 Steiner, *The Death of Tragedy*, pp. 7–8.

6 George Steiner, 'Tragedy, Pure and Simple', in *Tragedy and the Tragic: Greek Theatre and Beyond*, ed. Michael Silk (Oxford, 1996), pp. 534–46.

7 D. H. Lawrence, 'When I Read Shakespeare', in *Complete Poems* (Harmondsworth, 1993), pp. 494–5.

8 Friedrich Nietzsche, *Die fröhliche Wissenschaft*, in *Sämtliche Werke: Kritische Studienausgabe*, ed. G. Colli and M. Montinari, 15 vols (Berlin, 1988), Band 3, §80.

9 Steiner, *The Death of Tragedy*, p. 15.

10 Auden, *Lectures on Shakespeare*, p. 241.

11 William James, *The Varieties of Religious Experience* [1902] (Rockville, MD, 2008), p. 65.

12 Ibid., pp. 102–3.

13 Ibid., pp. 124–5.

FOUR Virtue, Happiness and Morality

1 Cf. Christine M. Korsgaard, *The Sources of Normativity* (Cambridge, 2003), p. 9.

2 Philippa Foot, 'Moral Beliefs', *Proceedings of the Aristotelian Society*, New Series (1958–9), p. 100.

3 Peter Geach, *The Virtues* (Cambridge, 1977), p. 17.

4 Rosalind Hursthouse, 'Virtue Ethics', *Stanford Encyclopedia*

of Philosophy, www.plato.stanford.edu, accessed 9 December 2014.

5 Alasdair MacIntyre, *After Virtue: A Study in Moral Theory* (London, 1981).

6 Rosalind Hursthouse, *On Virtue Ethics* (Oxford, 1999).

7 Aristotle, *Nicomachean Ethics* [350 BC], trans. David Ross (Oxford, 2009), 1124b9–1125a16.

8 My argument that follows is indebted to Timothy Chappell, 'Eudaimonia, Happiness and the Redemption of Unhappiness', *Philosophical Topics*, XXXI/1 (2013), pp. 27–52.

9 Aristotle, *Nicomachean Ethics*, 1099a6–7.

10 Raymond Geuss, 'Virtue and the Good Life', *Arion*, Third Series, VIII/1 (Spring/Summer 2000), p. 8.

11 Cf. Robin Barrow, *Happiness* (Oxford, 1980), p. 73.

12 Hermann Hesse, *Gertrud* [1910] (Frankfurt, 2006), p. 7.

13 Philippa Foot, 'Interview', *Philosophy Now*, www.philosophynow.org, accessed 9 December 2014.

14 F. R. Leavis, 'Memories of Wittgenstein', in *The Critic as Anti-philosopher: Essays and Papers*, ed. G. Singh (London, 1982), p. 135.

15 W. H. Auden, *The Dyer's Hand* [1948] (New York, 1962), p. 460.

16 Simone de Beauvoir, *Mémoires d'une jeune fille rangée* [1958] (Paris, 2013), p. 312.

17 Hursthouse, *On Virtue Ethics*, p. 187.

18 Ibid., p. 172.

19 Hannah Arendt, *The Human Condition* (Chicago, IL, 1958), p. 181.

20 Aristotle, *Nicomachean Ethics*, 1101a5–7; 1100a7–8.

21 Bernard Williams, *The Sense of the Past: Essays in the History of Philosophy*, ed. and intro. M. Burnyeat (Princeton, NJ, 2006), p. 178.

22 Philippa Foot, *Natural Goodness* (Oxford, 2001), p. 97.

23 Hursthouse, *On Virtue Ethics*, p. 173.

24 Jonathan Lear, *Happiness, Death and the Remainder of Life* (Cambridge, MA, 2002).

25 Foot, *Natural Goodness*, pp. 94ff.

26 Nietzsche, *Jenseits von Gut und Böse*, in *Sämtliche Werke: Kritische Studienausgabe*, ed. G. Colli and M. Montinari, 15 vols (Berlin, 1988), Band 5, §39.

27 Beauvoir, *Mémoires d'une jeune fille rangée*, p. 23.

28 Bernard Williams, 'The Women of Trachis: Fictions, Pessimism, Ethics', in The Greeks and Us: Essays in Honor of W. H. Adkins, ed. Robert B. Louden and Paul Schollmeier (Chicago, IL, 1996), pp. 48, 43, 52, 51.

29 Heinrich von Kleist, Michael Kohlhaas, in Sämtliche Werke und Briefe (Munich, 1994), Band 2, pp. 9–103.

30 Nietzsche, Die Geburt der Tragödie, in Sämtliche Werke: Kritische Studienausgabe, ed. G. Colli and M. Montinari, 15 vols (Berlin, 1988), Band 1, §7.

31 Albert Camus, Les Justes [1949] (Paris, 2014), Act 3, p. 90.

32 Henry Staten, Nietzsche's Voice (Ithaca, NY, 1993), pp. 78–9.

33 La Rochefoucauld, Maximes [1659] (Paris, 1977), no. 182.

34 W. H. Auden, Secondary Worlds (London, 1968), p. 118.

35 George Orwell, 'Why I Write', in The Penguin Essays of George Orwell (Harmondsworth, 1984), p. 9.

36 C. S. Lewis, A Grief Observed (London, 1966), p. 16.

37 Ibid., p. 52.

38 Ibid., p. 36.

39 Iris Murdoch, The Sovereignty of Good (London, 1985), p. 84.

40 Arendt, The Human Condition, p. 77.

41 Williams, The Sense of the Past, p. 44.

42 Hannah Arendt, Responsibility and Judgment, ed. Jerome Kohn (New York, 2003), p. 50.

43 Stefan Zweig, Die Welt von Gestern [1944] (Frankfurt, 1999), p. 459.

44 Arendt, Responsibility and Judgment, p. 50.

45 Jean Améry, Jenseits von Schuld und Sühne [1966] (Stuttgart, 2008), p. 32.

46 Hannah Arendt, Responsibility and Judgment, pp. 54–5.

47 J. S. Mill, On Bentham and Coleridge [1838; 1840] (London, 1971), p. 62.

48 Simone Weil, 'La Personne et le sacré', in Écrits de Londres et dernières lettres (Paris, 1957), pp. 11–44.

49 Jean-Paul Sartre, Existentialism and Humanism [1946], trans. Philip Mairet (London, 1989), p. 40.

FIVE Among the Ruins

1 Søren Kierkegaard, Fear and Trembling [1843], trans. Sylvia Walsh (Cambridge, 2006), p. 3.

2   D. H. Lawrence, *Lady Chatterley's Lover* [1928] (Harmondsworth, 1994), p. 5.

3   La Rochefoucauld, *Maximes* [1659] (Paris, 1977), no. 22.

4   Samuel Johnson, *The History of Rasselas, Prince of Abissinia* [1759] (Harmondsworth, 1985), pp. 179–81.

5   Nietzsche, *Morgenröthe*, in *Sämtliche Werke: Kritische Studienausgabe*, ed. G. Colli and M. Montinari, 15 vols (Berlin, 1988), Band 3, §534.

6   Richard Dawkins, *The God Delusion* (London, 2006), p. 307.

7   Primo Levi, *I sommersi e i salvati* (Torino, 2009), p. 110.

8   Albert Camus, 'Noces à Tipasa', in *Noces; (suivi de) l'Été* [1959] (Paris, 2015), pp. 16–17.

9   Henry David Thoreau, *Walden* [1854], ed. Stephen Fender (Oxford, 2008), p. 9.

10 W. Somerset Maugham, *The Summing Up* [1938] (London, 1944), pp. 57–8.

six Some Final Thoughts

1   Philip Larkin, 'Church Going', in *The Less Deceived* [1955] (Hull, 1977), pp. 28–9.

2   Sigmund Freud, *Three Essays on the Theory of Sexuality*, in *On Sexuality* [1905] (Harmondsworth, 1991), p. 61.

3   Simone de Beauvoir, *Mémoires d'une jeune fille rangée* (Paris, 2013), p. 312.

BIBLIOGRAPHY

*For texts in languages other than English, I provide in each case details
of a readily available English translation, where such exists.*

Adorno, Theodor, *Minima Moralia: Reflections from Damaged Life*
    [1951], trans. E.F.N. Jephcott (London, 1987)
Améry, Jean, *Jenseits von Schuld und Sühne* [1966] (Stuttgart,
    2008) [English translation: *At the Mind's Limits*, trans. Sidney
    Rosenfeld and Stella P. Rosenfeld (Bloomington, IN, 2009)]
Arendt, Hannah, *The Human Condition* (Chicago, IL, 1958)
—, *Responsibility and Judgment*, ed. Jerome Kohn (New York,
    2003)
Auden, W. H., *The Dyer's Hand* [1948] (New York, 1962)
—, *Lectures on Shakespeare*, ed. Arthur Kirsch (Princeton, NJ,
    2000)
—, *Secondary Worlds* (London, 1968)
Baudelaire, Charles, 'Anywhere out of the World: N'importe où
    hors du monde', in *Le Spleen de Paris: Petits poèmes en prose*
    [1869] (Paris, 2003), pp. 205–7 [English translation: *Paris
    Spleen*, trans. Louise Varèse (New York, 1970)]
Beauvoir, Simone de, *Mémoires d'une jeune fille rangée* [1958]
    (Paris, 2013) [English translation: *Memoirs of a Dutiful
    Daughter*, trans. James Kirkup (Harmondsworth, 2001)]
Borges, Jorge Luis, 'Borges y yo', in *Narraciones* (Barcelona, 1982),
    pp. 155–6 [English translation: in *Labyrinths*, trans. Donald
    A. Yates and James E. Irby (Harmondsworth, 2000),
    pp. 282–3]
Bradley, A. C., 'Hegel's Theory of Tragedy' [1909], in *Oxford
    Lectures on Poetry* (New York, 1999), pp. 69–98
Calder, John, *The Philosophy of Samuel Beckett* (London, 2001)

Camus, Albert, *Les Justes* [1949] (Paris, 2014) [English translation: in *Caligula and Other Plays*, trans. Henry Jones (Harmondsworth, 2006), pp. 163–228]

—, *Noces; (suivi de) l'Été* [1959] (Paris, 2015) [English translation: in *Lyrical and Critical Essays*, ed. Philip Tody, trans. Ellen Conroy Kennedy (New York, 1985), pp. 63–181]

Cioran, Emil, *De l'inconvénient d'être né* [1973] (Paris, 2009) [English translation: *The Trouble with Being Born*, trans. Richard Howard (New York, 2013)]

Critchley, Simon, 'Phaedra's Malaise', in *Rethinking Tragedy*, ed. Rita Felski (Baltimore, MD, 2008), pp. 170–95

Dawkins, Richard, *The God Delusion* (London, 2006)

Dienstag, Joshua Foa, *Pessimism* (Princeton, NJ, 2006)

Eagleton, Terry, 'Commentary', in *Rethinking Tragedy*, ed. Rita Felski (Baltimore, MD, 2008), pp. 337–46

Eliot, T. S., *The Cocktail Party* [1949] (London, 1982)

Fitzgerald, F. Scott, *The Great Gatsby*, ed. and intro. Tony Tanner [1925] (Harmondsworth, 2000)

Foot, Philippa, 'Moral Beliefs', in *Proceedings of the Aristotelian Society*, LIX (1958–9), pp. 83–104

—, *Natural Goodness* (Oxford, 2001)

Freud, Sigmund, *Three Essays on the Theory of Sexuality*, in *On Sexuality* [1905], trans. Angela Richards (Harmondsworth, 1991), pp. 45–161

Geach, Peter, *The Virtues* (Cambridge, 1977)

Geuss, Raymond, 'Virtue and the Good Life', *Arion*, 3rd series, VIII/1 (Spring/Summer 2000), pp. 1–24

Harper, Margaret Mills, 'Yeats and the Occult', in *The Cambridge Companion to W. B. Yeats*, ed. Marjorie Howes and John Kelly (Cambridge, 2006), pp. 144–66

Heller, Erich, *Kafka* (London, 1977)

Hesse, Hermann, *Gertrud* [1910] (Frankfurt, 2006) [English translation: *Gertrude*, trans. Adele Lewisohn (Claremont, CA, 2012)]

Hursthouse, Rosalind, *On Virtue Ethics* (Oxford, 1999)

—, 'Virtue Ethics', in *Stanford Encyclopedia of Philosophy*, www.plato.stanford.edu, accessed 9 December 2014

James, William, 'The Present Dilemma in Philosophy' [1907], in *Pragmatism and Other Writings* (Harmondsworth, 2000), pp. 7–23

—, *The Varieties of Religious Experience* [1902] (Rockville, MD, 2008)

Johnson, Samuel, *The History of Rasselas, Prince of Abissinia*
    [1759], ed. D. J. Enright (Harmondsworth, 1985)
Josipovici, Gabriel, *Contre-Jour* (Manchester, 1986)
—, *Touch* (New Haven, CT, 1996)
Kierkegaard, Søren, *Fear and Trembling* [1843], trans. Sylvia Walsh
    (Cambridge, 2006)
Kleist, Heinrich von, *Michael Kohlhaass*, in *Sämtliche Werke und*
    Briefe (Munich, 1994), Band 2, pp. 9–103 [English translation:
    in: '*The Marquise of O–' and Other Stories*, trans. David Luke
    and Nigel Reeves (Harmondsworth, 1978), pp. 114–213]
Korsgaard, Christine M., *The Sources of Normativity* (Cambridge,
    2003)
Lakoff, George, and Mark Johnson, *Metaphors We Live By*
    (Chicago, IL, 2003)
Larkin, Philip, 'An Interview with John Haffenden', in *Further*
    Requirements: Interviews, Broadcasts, Statements and Reviews,
    1952–1985, ed. Anthony Thwaite (London, 2002), pp. 47–64
—, *The Less Deceived* [1955] (Hull, 1977)
La Rochefoucauld, *Maximes* [1659] (Paris, 1977) [English
    translation: *Maxims*, trans. Leonard Tancock
    (Harmondsworth, 1981)]
Lawrence, D. H., *Lady Chatterley's Lover* [1928] (Harmondsworth,
    1994)
—, 'When I Read Shakespeare', in *Complete Poems*
    (Harmondsworth, 1993), pp. 494–5
Lear, Jonathan, *Happiness, Death and the Remainder of Life*
    (Cambridge, MA, 2002)
Leavis, F. R., 'Memories of Wittgenstein', in *The Critic as*
    Anti-philosopher: Essays and Papers, ed. G. Singh (London,
    1982), pp. 129–45
Levi, Primo, 'Jean Améry, il filosofo suicida', in *L'asimmetria e la*
    vita: articoli e saggi 1955–1987, ed. M. Belpoliti (Torino, 2002),
    pp. 70–72
—, *I sommersi e i salvati* [1986] (Torino, 2003) [English translation:
    The Drowned and the Saved, trans. Raymond Rosenthal
    (London, 1993)]
Lewis, C. S., *A Grief Observed* (London, 1966)
Lukács, Georg, *Soul and Form*, trans. Anna Bostock (London, 1980)
McGhee, Michael, *Transformations of Mind: Philosophy as Spiritual*
    Practice (Cambridge, 2000)
Márai, Sándor, *The Rebels*, trans. George Szirtes (New York, 2007)

Maugham, W. Somerset, *The Summing Up* [1938] (London, 1944)

Midgley, Mary, *Science and Poetry* (London, 2001)

Mill, J. S., *On Bentham and Coleridge* [1838; 1840], intro. by
F. R. Leavis (London, 1971)

Murdoch, Iris, *The Sovereignty of Good* (London, 1985)

Neiman, Susan, *Evil in Modern Thought* (Princeton, NJ, 2002)

Nietzsche, Friedrich, *Die fröhliche Wissenschaft*, in *Sämtliche
Werke: Kritische Studienausgabe*, 15 vols, 2nd edn, ed. G. Colli
and M. Montinari (Berlin, 1988), Band 3 [English translation:
The Gay Science, trans. Josefine Nauckhoff and Adrian del
Caro (Cambridge, 2001)]

—, *Die Geburt der Tragödie*, in *Sämtliche Werke: Kritische
Studienausgabe*, ed. G. Colli and M. Montinari, 15 vols,
2nd edn (Berlin, 1988), Band 1 [English translation: *The Birth
of Tragedy*, trans. Shaun Whiteside (Harmondsworth, 1993)]

—, *Jenseits von Gut und Böse*, in *Sämtliche Werke: Kritische
Studienausgabe*, ed. G. Colli and M. Montinari, 15 vols, 2nd
edn (Berlin, 1988), Band 5 [English translation: *Beyond Good
and Evil*, trans. R. J. Hollingdale (Harmondsworth, 2003)]

—, *Morgenröthe*, in *Sämtliche Werke: Kritische Studienausgabe*,
ed. G. Colli and M. Montinari, 15 vols, 2nd edn (Berlin,
1988), Band 3 [English translation: *Daybreak*, trans.
R. J. Hollingdale (Cambridge, 2003)]

Nozick, Robert, *Anarchy, State, and Utopia* (Oxford, 1974)

—, 'The Holocaust', in *The Examined Life* (New York, 1990),
pp. 236–42

—, *Philosophical Explanations* (Harvard, MA, 1981)

Nussbaum, Martha, *The Fragility of Goodness* (Cambridge, 1986)

Orwell, George, 'Benefit of Clergy: Some Notes on Salvador Dalí',
in *The Penguin Essays of George Orwell* (Harmondsworth,
1984), pp. 254–62

—, 'Why I Write', in *The Penguin Essays of George Orwell*
(Harmondsworth, 1984), pp. 7–13

Raine, Kathleen, *Autobiographies* (London, 1991)

Rhees, Rush, *On Religion and Philosophy*, ed. D. Z. Phillips
(Cambridge, 1997)

Rosenberg, Alan, and Gerald E. Meyers, eds, *Echoes from the
Holocaust: Philosophical Reflections in a Dark Time*
(Philadelphia, PA, 1988)

Sachs, Arieh, 'Samuel Johnson on "The Vacuity of Life"', *Studies in
English Literature, 1500–1900*, III/3 (Summer 1963), pp. 345–63

Sartre, Jean-Paul, *Existentialism and Humanism* [1946], trans.
Philip Mairet (London, 1989)

Sophocles, *Oedipus at Colonus*, in *The Theban Plays* [*c.* 401 BC],
trans. E. F. Watling (Harmondsworth, 1983)

Staten, Henry, *Nietzsche's Voice* (Ithaca, NY, 1993)

Steiner, George, *The Death of Tragedy* [1961] (New Haven, CT,
1996)

—, 'Tragedy, Pure and Simple', in *Tragedy and the Tragic: Greek
Theatre and Beyond*, ed. Michael Silk (Oxford, 1996),
pp. 534–46

Strawson, P. F., 'Social Morality and Individual Ideal', in *Freedom
and Resentment and Other Essays* (London, 1974)

Svevo, Italo, *La coscienza di Zeno* [1923] (Milan, 2011) [English
translation: *The Confessions of Zeno*, trans. Beryl de Zoete
(New York, 1989)]

Thoreau, Henry David, *Walden* [1854], ed. Stephen Fender
(Oxford, 2008)

Unamuno, Miguel de, *Del sentimiento trágico de la vida* [1913]
(Madrid, 2013) [English translation: *Tragic Sense of Life*, trans.
J. E. Crawford Flitch (New York, 1954)]

Weil, Simone, 'La Personne et le sacré', in *Écrits de Londres et
dernières lettres* (Paris, 1957), pp. 11–44 [English translation:
'On Human Personality', in David McLellan, *Simone Weil:
Utopian Pessimist* (London, 1989), pp. 273–88]

Williams, Bernard, *The Sense of the Past: Essays in the History of
Philosophy*, ed. M. Burnyeat (Princeton, NJ, 2006)

—, '"The Women of Trachis": Fictions, Pessimism, Ethics', in *The
Greeks and Us: Essays in Honor of W. H. Adkins*, ed. Robert B.
Louden and Paul Schollmeier (Chicago, IL, 1996), pp. 43–65

Williams, Raymond, *Modern Tragedy*, ed. Pamela McCallum
(Ontario, 2006)

Woolf, Virginia, *The Waves* [1931] (Oxford, 2008)

Zweig, Stefan, *Die Welt von Gestern* [1944] (Frankfurt, 1999)
[English translation: *The World of Yesterday*, trans. Anthea
Bell (London, 2011)]

ACKNOWLEDGEMENTS

I thank Sebastian Gardner, Michael Newton and Edith Steffen, whose friendship and conversation have done so much to form my view of life.

I am deeply grateful to Nelly Mars for her support in so many ways while I devoted myself to writing an impossible book.

I thank my students at King's College London for their exploration with me of many of the themes discussed in this work. I am also grateful for the responses to my ideas from the participants in the West London Philosophy group and to various other audiences to whom I presented some of the thoughts explored in this book, especially those at the University of Salzburg, Austria, and at the University of Trent, Italy.

I am particularly grateful to Ben Hayes at Reaktion Books for his patience, support and faith in this project, without which it would never have been completed.

I thank my university, King's College London, for allowing me the research time away from the demands of teaching and administration during which I was able to write much of this book.

I wrote this book in three cities, all of which have in their different ways contributed to my ideas: Bologna, because its elegance is so consoling; Madrid, because it knows how to throw itself into all it does; and London, because all of life is there.